R. Gupta's®

RRB

Railway Recruitment Board

Assistant Loco Pilot (ALP)
Technicians

FIRST STAGE COMPUTER BASED TEST (CBT)
(COMMON FOR ALP/TECHNICIAN)

10

PRACTICE PAPERS
(Solved)

2019
EDITION

Ramesh Publishing House, New Delhi

Published by
O.P. Gupta *for* Ramesh Publishing House

Admin. Office
12-H, New Daryaganj Road, Opp. Officers' Mess,
New Delhi-110002 ① 23261567, 23275224, 23275124

E-mail: info@rameshpublishinghouse.com
Website: www.rameshpublishinghouse.com

Showroom
● Balaji Market, Nai Sarak, Delhi-6 ① 23253720, 23282525
● 4457, Nai Sarak, Delhi-6, ① 23918938

Book Code: R-1958

ISBN: 978-93-87604-44-5

HSN Code: 49011010

Contents

● ● ●

SCHEME OF EXAM

First Stage Computer Based Test (CBT)

(Common For ALP/TECHNICIAN)

Duration : 60 Minutes

No. of Questions : 75

The First State CBT is of screening nature and the standard of questions for the CBT will be generally in conformity with the educational standards and/or minimum technical qualifications prescribed for the posts. The score of first stage exam shall be used only for short listing of candidates for second stage exam as per their merit.

The Questions will be of objective type with multiple choices and are likely to include questions pertaining to:

- **Mathematics**
- **General Intelligence and Reasoning**
- **General Science**
- **General Awareness and Current Affairs**

R. Gupta's® Useful Book for This Exam

Popular Master Guide
RRB-Assistant Loco Pilot/Technicians
First Stage CBT (Common for ALP/Technician)

- Specialised Study & Practice Material Prepared by Experts
- Numerous Solved Multiple Choice Questions

RAMESH PUBLISHING HOUSE

12-H, New Daryaganj Road, Delhi-110002
For Online Shopping: www.rameshpublishinghouse.com

10 Practice Papers

(Solved)

RRB—Railway Recruitment Board
Assistant Loco Pilot (ALP) & Technicians,
Recruitment Examination

FIRST STAGE COMPUTER BASED TEST (CBT)

1. If $x - \dfrac{1}{x} = 9$, then $x^2 + \dfrac{1}{x^2}$ is
   A. 83
   B. 81
   C. 79
   D. 72

2. The value of $\dfrac{\sqrt{32} + \sqrt{48}}{\sqrt{8} + \sqrt{12}}$ is
   A. 2
   B. $\sqrt{2}$
   C. 4
   D. 8

3. A 15 m high, vertical straight tree gets broken by the wind in such a way that its top touches the ground making an angle of 60° from the ground. At what height did the tree break?
   A. 5.96 m
   B. 5.19 m
   C. 6.96 m
   D. 6.19 m

4. The value of sec A (1 – sin A) (sec A + tan A) is
   A. –1
   B. 1
   C. 2
   D. $\dfrac{1}{2}$

5. The value of $\dfrac{5\cos^2 60° + 4\sec^2 30° - \tan^2 45°}{\sin^2 30° + \cos^2 30°}$ is
   A. $\dfrac{37}{12}$
   B. $\dfrac{47}{12}$
   C. $\dfrac{57}{12}$
   D. $\dfrac{67}{12}$

6. Second and third terms of an A.P. are 14 and 18 respectively. The sum of its first 51 terms is
   A. 5610
   B. 5614
   C. 5606
   D. 5618

7. The mean of first 8 prime numbers is
   A. 7.425
   B. 8.625
   C. 9.625
   D. 10.425

8. A fair coin is tossed 100 times and head occurs 58 times and tail occurs 42 times. The experimental probability of getting a head is
   A. $\dfrac{50}{100}$
   B. $\dfrac{42}{100}$
   C. $\dfrac{58}{100}$
   D. $\dfrac{42}{58}$

9. The sides of a triangle are 13 cm, 14 cm and 15 cm. The area is
   A. 42 cm^2
   B. 21 cm^2
   C. 63 cm^2
   D. 84 cm^2

10. A toy is in the form of a cone of radius 3.5 cm mounted on a hemisphere of same radius. The total height of the toy is 15.5 cm. Total surface area of the toy is
    A. 214.5 cm^2
    B. 146.5 cm^2
    C. 324.5 cm^2
    D. 114.5 cm^2

11. Three metallic spheres of radii 6 cm, 8 cm and 10 cm respectively, are melted and recast to form a solid sphere. The radius of this sphere is
    A. 8 cm
    B. 10 cm
    C. 12 cm
    D. 14 cm

12. Area of a quadrant of a circle whose circumference is 22 cm is
    A. $\dfrac{77}{4}$ cm^2
    B. $\dfrac{77}{8}$ cm^2
    C. $\dfrac{154}{3}$ cm^2
    D. $\dfrac{154}{6}$ cm^2

13. A train travels 360 km at a uniform speed. By increasing its speed by 5 km/hr it takes one hour less for the same journey. The original speed of the train is
    A. 45 km/hr
    B. 40 km/hr
    C. 50 km/hr
    D. 60 km/hr

14. Ratio of the ages of a father and son at present 2 : 1. Fifteen years back it was 3 : 1. The present age of the father is
    A. 70 years
    B. 65 years
    C. 55 years
    D. 60 years

15. Passing marks in an examination are 40%. A student obtains 200 marks and fails by 40 marks. The total marks for the examination are
    A. 600
    B. 550
    C. 500
    D. 450

16. In a mixture of 60 kg, the ratio of cement and sand is 3 : 1. Another 15 kg of cement is added to the mixture. The ratio of cement and sand now is
    A. 1 : 4
    B. 3 : 2
    C. 4 : 1
    D. 2 : 3

17. There are 400 children in a children's home. If each one is given 200 gm of ration daily, it is enough for 30 days. 100 more children join the home and ration intake is reduced to 150 gm per day. The ration will be sufficient for
    A. 30 days
    B. 32 days
    C. 35 days
    D. 40 days

18. Abdul has purchased a cycle for ₹ 4,176. The manufacturer earns a profit of 16 per cent and both wholesaler and retailer earn profit at the rate of 20 per cent each. The manufacturer's cost price is
    A. ₹ 3,200
    B. ₹ 3,000
    C. ₹ 2,700
    D. ₹ 2,500

Directions (Qs. 19 to 23): *Six persons A, B, C, D, E and F participated in a debate. Out of the six persons two were ladies; E and his unmarried sister were new entrants this year in the debate; husband of D was winner of last year and participated in this year's debate; A and C were runner-up last year; this year's winner was neither a new entrant nor winner of last year; B left the debate in the middle for some unavoidable reason; at the end of the debate, C secured more points than A but less than E and F.*

On the basis of above information answer the following questions:

19. Who is the husband of D?
    A. A
    B. B
    C. E
    D. C

20. Who was the winner last year?
    A. A
    B. B
    C. D
    D. E

21. Who is the sister of E?
    A. C
    B. D
    C. F
    D. A

22. Who was the winner in the debate this year?
    A. B
    B. C
    C. D
    D. A

23. Find the missing number.

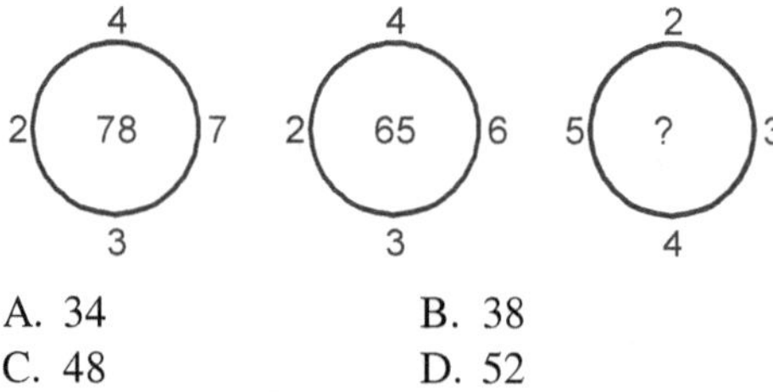

    A. 34
    B. 38
    C. 48
    D. 52

Directions (Qs. 24 to 27): *In each of the following questions an incomplete series of numbers with one blank is given. Identify the missing number from the given alternatives.*

24. 1, 8, 27, 64, ?, 216
    A. 85
    B. 125
    C. 155
    D. 205

25. 2, 11, 38, 119, ?
    A. 357
    B. 380
    C. 362
    D. 418

26. 4, 15, 37, 70, ?, 169
    A. 103
    B. 106
    C. 117
    D. 114

27. 29, 54, 103, 200, 393, ?

    A. 586   B. 490

    C. 678   D. 778

28. Which pair is different in some way from others in the following?

    A. Milk – Butter

    B. Inkpot – Ink

    C. Sugarcane – Sugar

    D. Coconut – Oil

29. If 'Family' is coded as 316459 and 'Sister' is coded as 747820, then 'Mystery' will be coded as

    A. 6987209   B. 6798209

    C. 6978209   D. 6972809

30. If GIRL is coded as HHJJQQNN, then FOND will be coded as

    A. GGPPMMEE   B. GGPPMMFF

    C. GGNNMMFF   D. GGPPNNFF

Directions (Qs. 31 to 35): *Read the following paragraph to answer questions that follow:*

A and B play Football and Hockey. C and E play Tennis and Cricket. A and D play Tennis and Volleyball. B and E play Cricket. C and E play Volleyball. C and D play Hockey. D and E play Football and Cricket.

31. Who does *not* play Cricket?

    A. A   B. B

    C. C   D. E

32. Who plays Football, Hockey and Tennis?

    A. D   B. C

    C. B   D. E

33. Who plays only Tennis, Cricket, Volleyball and Hockey?

    A. A   B. B

    C. C   D. D

34. Who plays only Football, Hockey and Cricket?

    A. A   B. B

    C. C   D. D

35. Who plays all these games except Hockey?

    A. B   B. E

    C. D   D. C

Directions (Qs. 36): *Read the following paragraph to answer the question that follow:*

A, B, C, D, E all have six balls. B gives two balls to E who gives one ball to D. A gives four balls to C who gives two balls to B. B gives three balls to D, who gives one ball to A.

36. How many balls does B have?

    A. 2   B. 8

    C. 7   D. 3

37. Which of the following is *not* a physical change?

    A. Boiling of water to give water vapour

    B. Melting of ice to give liquid water

    C. Dissolution of salt in water

    D. Combustion of Liquefied Petroleum Gas (LPG)

38. Which of the following gives the correct increasing order or acidic strength?

    A. Water < Acetic acid < Hydrochloric acid

    B. Water < Hydrochloric acid < Acetic acid

    C. Acetic acid < Water < Hydrochloric acid

    D. Hydrochloric acid < Water < Acetic acid

39. The ability of metals to be drawn into thin wires is known as

    A. ductility

    B. malleability

    C. sonorosity

    D. conductivity

40. Gunmetal contains

    A. Cu = 60%, Sn = 40%

    B. Cu = 80%, Sn = 20%

    C. Cu = 70%, Sn = 30%

    D. Cu = 90%, Sn = 10%

41. MRI stands for

    A. Magnets Resonant Imaging

    B. Magnetic Resonance Imaging

    C. Magnetic Radar Imaging

    D. Magnet Radial Imaging

42. What is the maximum resistance which can be made using five resistors each of $\frac{1}{5}\,\Omega$?

A. $\frac{1}{5}\,\Omega$ B. 10 W

C. 5 W   D. 1 W

43. Which of the following is *not* associated with growth of plants?
A. Auxins   B. Gibberellins
C. Cytokinins   D. Abscisic acid

44. In a neuron, conversion of electrical signal to a chemical signal occurs at/in
A. cell body   B. axonal end
C. dendritic end   D. axon

45. Drinking alcohol is very harmful and it ruins the health. 'Drinking alcohol' stands for
A. drinking methyl alcohol
B. drinking ethyl alcohol
C. drinking propyl alcohol
D. drinking isopropyl alcohol

46. Which of the following elements does *not* lose an electron easily?
A. Mg   B. Na
C. K   D. Ca

47. Length of pollen tube depends on the distance between
A. pollen grain and upper surface of stigma
B. pollen grain on upper surface of stigma and ovule
C. pollen grain in anther and upper surface of stigma
D. upper surface of stigma and lower part of style

48. Gonorrhoea is caused by a bacterium called
A. *Neisseria gonorrhoeae*
B. *Treponema pallidum*
C. *Lactobacillus*
D. *Streptococcus*

49. Which of the following is *not* a natural resource?
A. Soil   B. Water
C. Electricity   D. Air

50. Which of the following is a 'biodiversity hot spot'?
A. Rivers   B. Forests
C. Deserts   D. Oceans

51. Depletion of ozone is mainly due to
A. chlorofluorocarbon   B. carbon monoxide
C. methane   D. pesticides

52. Which group of organisms are *not* constituents of a food chain?
A. Grass, lion, rabbit
B. Plankton, man, fish, grasshopper
C. Wolf, grass, snake, tiger
D. Frog, snake, eagle, grass, grasshopper

53. Red light is used for danger signal as
A. it has higher wavelength
B. it can travel large distance
C. it scatters the least
D. it scatters the longest

54. Twinkling of stars is due to atmospheric
A. dispersion of light by water droplets
B. refraction of light by different layers of varying refractive indices
C. scattering of light by dust particles
D. internal reflection of light by clouds

55. Which unit of valuation is known as 'Paper Gold'?
A. Petrodollar
B. SDR
C. Eurodollar
D. GDR

56. The coastline that borders the state of Kerala, is known as
A. Konkan Coast
B. Malabar Coast
C. Coromandel Coast
D. Canara Coast

57. Who is the founder of World Economic Forum?
A. Klaus Schwab
B. John Kenneth Galbraith
C. Robert Zoellick
D. Paul Krugman

58. The concept of sustainable development relates to
A. Consumption levels
B. Exhaustible levels
C. Social equity
D. None of these

59. Article-17 of the Constitution provides for
A. Equality before law
B. Equality of opportunity in matters of public employment
C. Abolition of titles
D. Abolition of untouchability

60. Where did the practice of 'Shadow Cabinet' originate?
A. USA
B. Great Britain
C. Italy
D. France

61. The Indian Citizenship Act was passed in
A. 1950
B. 1952
C. 1955
D. 1960

62. Saka Era which starts from 78 AD represents
A. Kanishka's reign
B. Prosperity of Harsha
C. Shivaji's reign
D. Chandragupta's reign

63. The foundation stone of the Gateway of India was laid in
A. 1911
B. 1927
C. 1857
D. 1947

64. Almatti Dam is located on which of the following rivers?
A. Godavari
B. Kaveri
C. Krishna
D. Mahanadi

65. Which of the following are the youngest mountains of India?
A. Aravallis
B. Himalayas
C. Nilgiris
D. Vindhyachal

66. Gresham's law in Economics relates to
A. Supply and demand
B. Circulation of currency
C. Consumption of supply
D. Distribution of goods and services

67. Revealed Preference Theory was propounded by
A. Adam Smith
B. Marshall
C. P.A. Samuelson
D. J.S. Mill

68. The Indian Independence League was set up by
A. Rash Behari Bose
B. S.M. Joshi
C. Aruna Asaf Ali
D. Jai Prakash Narayan

69. The description of Caste System is found in
A. Rig Veda
B. Sam Veda
C. Yajur Veda
D. None of these

70. The capital of Pallavas was
A. Arcot
B. Kanchi
C. Malkhed
D. Banaras

71. In early medieval India, what did the term 'Jital' refer to?
A. Weight
B. Diet
C. Coin
D. Game

72. Which of the following is *not* a Kharif crop?
A. Rice
B. Groundnut
C. Maize
D. Barley

73. 'Bluetooth' which is common in mobile phones gets its name from:
A. Danish 10th Century King
B. U.K. Software Company
C. Greek Goddess
D. Sony

74. The 'Pulitzer Prize' is associated with:
A. Environmental protections
B. Civil Aviation
C. Journalism
D. Health Research

75. The layer of the atmosphere which provides ideal flying conditions for large jet Aero plane:
A. Ionosphere
B. Exosphere
C. Troposphere
D. Stratosphere

ANSWERS

1	2	3	4	5	6	7	8	9	10
A	A	C	B	D	A	C	C	D	A

11	12	13	14	15	16	17	18	19	20
C	B	B	D	A	C	B	D	B	B

21	22	23	24	25	26	27	28	29	30
C	C	D	B	C	D	D	B	C	B

31	32	33	34	35	36	37	38	39	40
A	A	C	B	B	D	D	A	A	D

41	42	43	44	45	46	47	48	49	50
B	D	D	B	B	A	C	A	C	B

51	52	53	54	55	56	57	58	59	60
A	C	C	B	B	B	A	B	D	B

61	62	63	64	65	66	67	68	69	70
C	A	A	C	B	B	C	A	A	B

71	72	73	74	75
C	D	A	C	D

EXPLANATORY ANSWERS

1. $\because\ x - \dfrac{1}{x} = 9$

squaring both sides,

$$x^2 + \dfrac{1}{x^2} - 2 = (9)^2$$

$$\therefore\quad x^2 + \dfrac{1}{x^2} = 81 + 2 = 83.$$

2. $\dfrac{\sqrt{32} + \sqrt{48}}{\sqrt{8} + \sqrt{12}} = \dfrac{4\sqrt{2} + 4\sqrt{3}}{2\sqrt{2} + 2\sqrt{3}}$

$$= \dfrac{4\left(\sqrt{2} + \sqrt{3}\right)}{2\left(\sqrt{2} + \sqrt{3}\right)} = 2$$

3.

$$\cos 60° = \dfrac{x}{h}$$

$$\Rightarrow\quad \dfrac{1}{2} = \dfrac{x}{h}$$

$$\Rightarrow\quad h = 2x$$

$$\Rightarrow\quad x = \dfrac{h}{2}$$

$$\tan 60° = \dfrac{15 - h}{x}$$

$$\Rightarrow\quad \sqrt{3} = \dfrac{15 - h}{x}$$

$$\Rightarrow\quad \sqrt{3}\,x = 15 - h$$

$$\Rightarrow\quad \sqrt{3} \times \dfrac{h}{2} = 15 - h$$

$$\Rightarrow\quad \sqrt{3}\,h = 30 - 2h$$

$$2h + \sqrt{3}\,h = 30$$

$$h\left(2 + \sqrt{3}\right) = 30$$

$$\Rightarrow \qquad h = \frac{30}{2+\sqrt{3}}$$

$$\Rightarrow \qquad h = \frac{30}{2+\sqrt{3}} \times \frac{2-\sqrt{3}}{2-\sqrt{3}}$$

$$= \frac{30(2-1.732)}{4-3}$$

$$= 30 \times \frac{268}{1000} = \frac{804}{100} = 8.04$$

$$\therefore \ 15 - h = 15 - 8.04 = 6.96 \text{ m.}$$

4. sec A $(1 - \sin A)$ (sec A + tan A)

$\Rightarrow$ (sec A $-$ sec A . sin A) (sec A + tan A)

$= $ (sec A $-$ tan A) (sec A + tan A)

$= \sec^2 - \tan^2 A = 1.$

5.
$$\frac{5 \times \left(\frac{1}{2}\right)^2 + 4\left(\frac{2}{\sqrt{3}}\right)^2 - 1}{1}$$

$$[\because \ \sin^2\theta + \cos^2\theta = 1]$$

$$= 5 \times \frac{1}{4} + 4 \times \frac{4}{3} - 1$$

$$= \frac{5}{4} + \frac{16}{3} - 1 = \frac{15 + 64 - 12}{12}$$

$$= \frac{64 + 3}{12} = \frac{67}{12}.$$

6. Let first term of AP is a and common difference $= d$

$$a + d = 14 \qquad\qquad ...(i)$$
$$a + 2d = 18 \qquad\qquad ...(ii)$$

Subtract (i) from (ii) we get

$d = 4$ and $a = 10$

$$\because \qquad S_n = \frac{n}{2}\{2a + (n-1)d\}$$

$$\therefore \qquad S_{51} = \frac{51}{2}\{2 \times 10 + (50) \times 4\}$$

$$= \frac{51}{2}\{20 + 200\}$$

$$= 51 \times 110$$

$$= 5610$$

7. First 8 prime numbers are

2, 3, 5, 7, 11, 13, 17, 19

$$\text{Mean} = \frac{2+3+5+7+11+13+17+19}{8}$$

$$= \frac{77}{8} = 9.625.$$

9. $S = \dfrac{a+b+c}{2} = \dfrac{13+14+15}{2} = \dfrac{42}{2} = 21$

Area of $\Delta = \sqrt{s(s-a)(s-b)(s-c)}$

$$= \sqrt{21 \times 8 \times 7 \times 6}$$

$$= \sqrt{3 \times 7 \times 2 \times 2 \times 2 \times 7 \times 3 \times 2}$$

$$= 3 \times 7 \times 2 \times 2 = 84 \text{ cm}^2.$$

10. Height of cone $= 15.5 - 3.5 = 12$ cm

$$\text{Slant height} = \sqrt{\left(\frac{7}{2}\right)^2 + (12)^2} = \sqrt{\frac{625}{4}}$$

$$= \frac{25}{2} \text{ cm}$$

C.S.A of cone $= \pi r l = \dfrac{22}{7} \times \dfrac{7}{2} \times \dfrac{25}{2} = \dfrac{275}{2}$ cm^2

C.S.A of hemisphere $= 2\pi r^2$

$$= 2 \times \frac{22}{7} \times \frac{7}{2} \times \frac{7}{2} = 77 \text{ cm}^2$$

$\therefore$ Total surface area of toy

$= 137.5 + 77 = 214.5$ cm^2.

11. According to the question,

$$\frac{4}{3}\pi R^3 = \frac{4}{3}\pi(6^3 + 8^3 + 10^3)$$

$$\Rightarrow \qquad R^3 = 216 + 512 + 1000$$
$$\Rightarrow \qquad R^3 = 1728$$
$$\therefore \qquad R = \sqrt[3]{1728} = 12 \text{ cm.}$$

12. $C = 2\pi r$

$$\Rightarrow \qquad 22 = 2 \times \frac{22}{7} \times r \ \Rightarrow r = \frac{7}{2} \text{ cm}$$

Area of quadrant of a circle $= \dfrac{1}{4}\pi r^2$

$$= \frac{1}{4} \times \frac{22}{7} \times \frac{7}{2} \times \frac{7}{2} = \frac{77}{8} \text{ cm}^2.$$

13. Let the original speed = x km/hr

According to the question,

$$\frac{360}{x} - \frac{360}{x+5} = 1$$

$$\Rightarrow \quad \frac{360(x+5-x)}{x(x+5)} = 1$$

$$\Rightarrow \quad x^2 + 5x - 1800 = 0$$

$$\Rightarrow \quad (x - 40)(x + 45) = 0$$

$$\Rightarrow x = 40 \text{ or } x = -45$$

$\therefore$ Required speed = 40 km/hr.

14. Let present age of father = $2x$ years

son's age = x years

According to the question,

$$\frac{2x-15}{x-15} = \frac{3}{1}$$

$$\Rightarrow \quad 3x - 45 = 2x - 15$$

$$\Rightarrow \quad x = 30$$

$\therefore$ Father's present age = $2x = 2 \times 30$

$$= 60 \text{ years.}$$

15. Let total marks for the examination = x

$$40\% \text{ of } x = 200 + 40$$

$$\Rightarrow \quad \frac{40}{100} \times x = 240$$

$$\Rightarrow \quad x = \frac{240 \times 100}{40} = 600.$$

16. Amount of cement = $\frac{3}{4} \times 60 = 45$ kg

Amount of sand = $\frac{1}{4} \times 60 = 15$ kg

Now amount of cement = $45 + 15 = 60$ kg

$\therefore$ Required ratio = $\frac{60}{15} = \frac{4}{1} = 4 : 1$.

17. Required days = $\dfrac{400 \times 30 \times 200}{500 \times 150} = 32$

Hence, the ration will be sufficient = 32 days.

18. C.P. of retailer = $\dfrac{4176 \times 100}{120} = ₹\,3480$

C.P. of whole saler = $\dfrac{3480 \times 100}{120} = ₹\,2900$

$\therefore$ C.P. of manufacturer

$$= \frac{2900 \times 100}{116} = ₹\,2500$$

19-23. From given Datas:

F is E's sister and B is D's husband and as new entrant are not winner, so D is winner.

24.

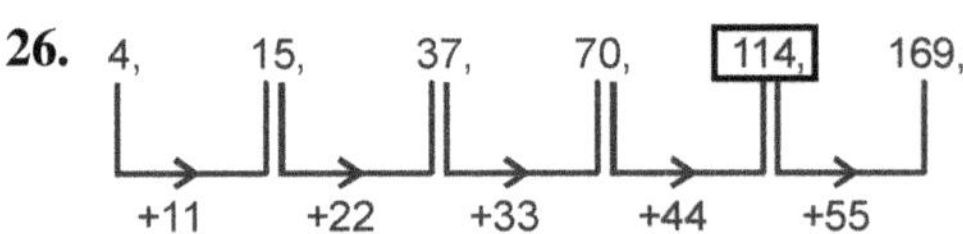

1,	8,	27,	64,	125,	216
$(1)^3$,	$(2)^3$,	$(3)^3$,	$(4)^3$,	$(5)^3$,	$(6)^3$,

25. 2, 11, 38, 119, 362,

$+3^2 \quad +3^3 \quad +3^4 \quad +3^5$

26. 4, 15, 37, 70, 114, 169,

$+11 \quad +22 \quad +33 \quad +44 \quad +55$

27. 29, 54, 103, 200, 393, 778,

$\times 2 - 4 \quad \times 2 - 5 \quad \times 2 - 6 \quad \times 2 - 7 \quad \times 2 - 8$

29. From given information:

Word	F	A	M	I	L	Y	S	I	S	T	E	R
Code	3	1	6	4	5	9	7	4	7	8	2	0

Hence, code for word Mystery is '6978209'.

31-35.

Football	Hockey	Tennis	Cricket	Volleyball
A, B,	A, B,	C, E,	B, C,	A, C,
D, E	C, D	A, D	D, E	D, E

RRB—Railway Recruitment Board

Assistant Loco Pilot (ALP) & Technicians,
Recruitment Examination

FIRST STAGE COMPUTER BASED TEST (CBT)

1. The value of $\left(a^{x-y}\right)^{x+y}\cdot\left(a^{y-z}\right)^{y+z}\cdot\left(a^{z-x}\right)^{z+x}$ is:
   A. 0
   B. 1
   C. –1
   D. $x + y + z$

2. The fifteenth part, the twelfth part and seventh part of a certain number when added together give 1353, the number is:
   A. 6150
   B. 6420
   C. 6240
   D. 4620

3. The value of $\dfrac{(0.035)^2 - (.0045)^2}{.0395}$ is:
   A. 0.0305
   B. 0.0395
   C. 0.0345
   D. 0.0354

4. An article which costs A ₹ 50 is sold to B at a profit of 20%; B sells it to C at a profit of 25%; C sells it to D at a profit of 40%. The price D paid for the article is:
   A. ₹ 147
   B. ₹ 105
   C. ₹ 85
   D. ₹ 95

5. The number which must be subtracted from 11, 15, 21 each so that the middle number so obtained is the mean proportional of the other two, is:
   A. 6
   B. 5
   C. 4
   D. 3

6. A sum of money put at compound interest amounts in 2 years to ₹ 3380 and in 3 years to ₹ 3515.20. The money invested is:
   A. ₹ 3125
   B. ₹ 3215
   C. ₹ 3512
   D. ₹ 3152

7. A pen is sold at ₹ 60.00 cash or ₹ 20.00 cash down payment and ₹ 8 per month for six months. The rate of interest is:
   A. 80%
   B. 100%
   C. 110%
   D. 120%

8. In an examination 77% candidates passed in English and 66% passed in Mathematics and 13% failed in both subjects. If 392 passed in both subjects the total number of candidates is:
   A. 500
   B. 600
   C. 700
   D. 800

9. A can do as much work in 2 days as B can do in 3 days, and B as much in 4 days as C in 5 days. If A, B and C together can do a piece of work in 5 days then A alone will do it in:
   A. 15 days
   B. 12 days
   C. 11 days
   D. 10 days

10. The value of $(1 + \cot\theta - \mathrm{cosec}\theta)\,(1 + \tan\theta + \sec\theta)$ is:
    A. 1
    B. –1
    C. 2
    D. –2

11. The value of $\sec70° \sin20° + \cos20° \,\mathrm{cosec}70°$ is:
    A. 1
    B. –1
    C. 2
    D. –2

12. The angles of elevation of the top of tower from two points a and b from the base and in the same straight line with it are complementary. The height of the tower is:
    A. $\sqrt{ab}$
    B. $\sqrt{\dfrac{a}{b}}$
    C. ab
    D. $\dfrac{a}{b}$

13. The difference between the sides at right angles in a right angled triangle is 14 cm. The area of the triangle is 120 cm². The perimeter of the triangle is:
    A. 26 cm
    B. 36 cm
    C. 54 cm
    D. 60 cm

14. The area of a square is the same as the area of a circle. Their perimeters are in the ratio:

A. $1 : 1$ B. $2 : \pi$

C. $\pi : 2$ D. $\sqrt{\pi} : 2$

15. The radii of two cylinders are in the ratio $2 : 3$ and their heights are in the ratio $5 : 3$. The ratio of their volumes is:

A. $27 : 20$ B. $20 : 27$

C. $4 : 9$ D. $9 : 4$

16. The circular ends of a bucket are of radii 35 cm and 14 cm and the height of the bucket is 40 cm. Its volume is:

A. 60060 cm^3 B. 80080 cm^3

C. 70040 cm^3 D. 80160 cm^3

17. The height (in cm) of 15 students of a class are

141, 151, 146, 155, 148, 150, 158, 147, 159, 152, 153, 149, 150, 160, 161.

The mean height is:

A. 152   B. 153

C. 152.5   D. 151

18. A bag contains 3 white, 4 red and 5 black balls. One ball is drawn at random. The probability that the ball drawn is neither black nor white is:

A. $\dfrac{1}{4}$ B. $\dfrac{1}{2}$

C. $\dfrac{1}{3}$ D. $\dfrac{2}{3}$

Directions (Qs. 19 to 23): *A and B play Hockey and Football. B and C play Cricket and Football. C and E play Cricket and Volleyball. D and E play tennis. A and C play Volleyball and Football. A and D play Hockey and Football.*

On the basis of above information answer the following questions:

19. Who does not play football?

A. B   B. C

C. D   D. E

20. Who plays Hockey, Football and Tennis?

A. E   B. D

C. C   D. A

21. Who plays Cricket, Hockey and Football?

A. A   B. C

C. B   D. E

22. Who plays Cricket, Volleyball and Tennis?

A. E   B. D

C. C   D. A

23. Who plays Hockey, Volleyball and Football?

A. A   B. B

C. C   D. E

24. If 'clock' is coded as 36938 and 'leave' is coded as 12452, then 'cave' should be coded as:

A. 4325   B. 3451

C. 3453   D. 3452

25. If 'sky' is coded as TTMMXX, then 'Lie' will be coded as:

A. MMLLDD   B. MMKKDD

C. MNOOCC   D. NNKKFF

26. If 'case' is coded as ECUG and 'Burn' is coded as CWTR. How 'earn' is encoded?

A. GDTP   B. HCTP

C. GCTR   D. GDPT

27. For every correct answer, a student scores one mark but for every incorrect answer she/he loses $\dfrac{1}{3}$ mark. She/He answered 108 questions but scored zero (0). How many questions she/he answered incorrectly?

A. 81   B. 78

C. 87   D. 72

Directions (Qs. 28 to 31): *Read the following paragraph to answer questions that follow:*

A, B, C, D, E all have nine marbles. B gives two marbles to D, who gives one marble to E. C gives 5 marbles to E who gives two marbles to A. C gives two marbles to B who gives three marble to E. D gives three marbles to A who gives two marbles to B.

28. How many marbles A has?

A. 7   B. 9

C. 10   D. 12

29. How many marbles B has?

A. 6   B. 7

C. 8   D. 10

30. How many marbles C has?
A. 3
B. 2
C. 6
D. 7

31. Now, who has got the maximum number of marbles?
A. B
B. C
C. D
D. E

Directions (Qs. 32 to 35): *A series of numbers is given, where one term is missing. Select the missing term from the given alternatives.*

32. 0, 3, 8, 15, 24, 35, _?_
A. 48
B. 46
C. 49
D. None of the above

33. 2, 9, 30, 93, 282, _?_
A. 746
B. 846
C. 849
D. 843

34. 24, 39, 416, 525, 636, _?_
A. 736
B. 749
C. 864
D. 849

35. 40, 29, _?_, 13, 8
A. 20
B. 18
C. 22
D. 17

Directions (Qs. 36): *In the following question, Three words are given. First word is related to the second word. You have to select from the given alternatives, the fourth word which would be related to the third word in similar way.*

36. Advocate : Law : : Cook : ?
A. Cooking
B. Kitchen
C. Food
D. Recipes

37. What happens, when zinc metal is dipped in copper sulphate solution?
A. the solution becomes colourless and reddish brown copper metal gets deposited
B. no reaction takes place
C. the solution becomes green and copper metal gets deposited
D. the solution remains blue and copper metal gets deposited

38. In binary fission of a cell:
A. Cytoplasm and nucleus divide at the same time.
B. The division of nucleus is followed by the division of cytoplasm.
C. The division of cytoplasm is followed by the division of nucleus.
D. The cytoplasm and nucleus do not divide.

39. When a cell is kept in a hypotonic solution then water moves:
A. into the cell
B. out of the cell
C. no movement of water takes place
D. none of these is correct

40. The isomers of C_6H_{14} are:
A. 4
B. 5
C. 6
D. 3

41. Which among the following diseases is ***not*** sexually transmitted?
A. Syphillis
B. Hepatitis
C. HIV-AIDS
D. Gonorrhoea

42. A full length image of a distant tall building can definitely be seen by using:
A. a concave mirror
B. a convex mirror
C. a plane mirror
D. both concave as well as plane mirror

43. The human eye forms the image of an object at its:
A. cornea
B. iris
C. pupil
D. retina

44. Which one of the following is an artificial ecosystem?
A. Pond
B. Crop field
C. Lake
D. Forest

45. Extensive plantation of trees to increase forest cover is known as:
A. Agro-forestry
B. Social forestry
C. Afforestation
D. Deforestation

46. Which of the following is an exothermic process?
A. Reaction of water with quicklime
B. Dilution of an acid
C. Evaporation of water
D. Sublimation of Camphor

47. Which among the following is ***not*** a base?
A. NaOH
B. KOH
C. NH_4OH
D. C_2H_5OH

48. Blood bank of the body is:
A. spleen   B. heart
C. liver   D. bone marrow

49. Electrical resistivity of a given metallic wire depends upon:
A. its length   B. its thickness
C. its shape   D. nature of material

50. Growth of the plant or plant parts towards the earth is called:
A. phototropism   B. hydrotropism
C. thigmotropism   D. geotropism

51. The unit of electric power may also be expressed as:
A. Volt ampere   B. Kilowatt hour
C. Watt second   D. Joule second

52. Biogas is a better fuel as it has:
A. 75% methane
B. higher calorific value
C. residual manure
D. All of these

53. Which of the following is different from the other three?
A. petroleum   B. coal
C. natural gas   D. geothermal

54. The centre for controlling body temperature is:
A. Hypothalamus
B. Cerebellum
C. Central nervous system
D. Cerebrum

55. Who was the Viceroy of India when Rowlatt Act passed?
A. Hardings II   B. Chelmsford
C. Simon   D. Minto II

56. The Vindhyan System of Rocks is important for the production of:
A. precious stones and building material
B. iron ore and managanese
C. bauxite and mica
D. copper and uranium

57. Which of the following acts gave representation to Indians for the first time in the legislature?
A. Indian Council Act, 1909
B. Indian Council Act, 1919
C. Govt. of India Act, 1935
D. Govt. of India Act, 1942

58. Which document was developed mentioning Samudragupta's Achievements?
A. Kalinga Edict   B. Hathigumpha Edict
C. Indica   D. Allahabad Prasasti

59. Which of the following Articles of the Directive Principles of State Policy deals with the promotion of International Peace and Security?
A. Article 51   B. Article 48A
C. Article 43A   D. Article 41

60. In which of the following matters does Lok Sabha has supremacy?
A. Railway Budget   B. Defence Budget
C. Foreign Affairs   D. Financial Bill

61. As per existing law what is the minimum per day wages paid to a worker from unorganised sector in India?
A. ₹ 50   B. ₹ 75
C. ₹ 100   D. ₹ 125

62. Who is the first law officer of the Govt. of India?
A. The Chief Justice of India
B. Union Law Minister
C. Attorney General of India
D. Law Secretary

63. Many a times we see in financial Journals / Bulletins a term M_3, what does the term M_3 mean?
A. Currency in circulation on a particular day
B. Total value of the foreign Exchange on a particular day
C. Total value of Export Credit on a given date
D. Total value of the tax collected in a year

64. Many a times we read in the newspapers that RBI has changed or revised a particular ratio /rate by a few base points. What is meant by base point?
A. Ten per cent of one hundredth point
B. One hundred of 1%

C. One hundred of 10%
D. Ten per cent of 1000

65. Nagarjuna Sagar Dam is built across the river:
A. Cauvery   B. Krishna
C. Narmada   D. Godavari

66. Firoz Shah founded many cities, which of the following was not built by him?
A. Jaunpur   B. Fatehpur Sikri
C. Hisar   D. Fatehabad

67. The Red Sea is an example of a:
A. folded structure   B. faulted structure
C. lava structure   D. residual structure

68. Isochrones are lines joining places with equal:
A. longitude
B. travelling time from a point
C. rainfall
D. frost

69. The pepper plant is a:
A. tree   B. vine
C. shrub   D. small herb

70. Which kind of power accounts for the largest share of power generation in India?
A. Hydro Electricity   B. Thermal
C. Nuclear   D. Solar

71. An image of dancing girl on the coins was found from:
A. Kalibangan   B. Harappa
C. Mohenjodara   D. Ropar

72. The Italian traveller who gave a very praise worthy account of the Vijaynagar Empire was:
A. Barbosa   B. Marco Polo
C. Nicolo Conti   D. Tome Pires

73. Who is the author of the book 'Imaging India':
A. Nandan Nilekani   B. Chetan Bhagat
C. Natwar Singh   D. Khuswant Singh

74. The latitude difference between India & Pakistan for their Standard time is:
A. 7°   B. 7.5°
C. 8°   D. 8.5°

75. Who among the following introduced the permanent Settlement of Bengal:
A. Warren Hastings
B. Lord Willam Bentinck
C. Lord Cornwallis
D. Lord Dalhousie

ANSWERS

1	2	3	4	5	6	7	8	9	10
B	D	A	B	D	A	D	C	C	C

11	12	13	14	15	16	17	18	19	20
C	A	D	D	B	B	A	C	D	B

21	22	23	24	25	26	27	28	29	30
C	A	A	D	B	C	A	D	C	B

31	32	33	34	35	36	37	38	39	40
D	A	C	B	A	D	A	A	B	B

41	42	43	44	45	46	47	48	49	50
B	B	D	A	C	A	D	A	D	D

51	52	53	54	55	56	57	58	59	60
B	D	D	A	B	A	C	D	A	D

61	62	63	64	65	66	67	68	69	70
C	A	A	A	B	B	C	B	B	D

71	72	73	74	75					
B	C	A	B	C					

EXPLANATORY ANSWERS

1. $\left(a^{x-y}\right)^{x+y} \cdot \left(a^{y-z}\right)^{y+z} \cdot \left(a^{z-x}\right)^{z+x}$

$= a^{x^2-y^2} \times a^{y^2-z^2} \times a^{z^2-x^2}$

$= a^{x^2-y^2+y^2-z^2+z^2-x^2} = a^0 = 1$

2. Let the number $= x$

According to the question,

$$\frac{x}{15}+\frac{x}{12}+\frac{x}{7} = 1353$$

$\Rightarrow \dfrac{28x+35x+60x}{420} = 1353$

$\Rightarrow \qquad 123x = 1353 \times 420$

$\Rightarrow \qquad x = \dfrac{1353 \times 420}{123}$

$\qquad\qquad = 11 \times 420 = 4620$

3. $\dfrac{(0.035)^2 - (0.0045)^2}{0.0395}$

$= \dfrac{(0.035 + 0.0045)(0.035 - 0.0045)}{0.0395}$

$= \dfrac{0.0395 \times (0.0305)}{0.0395}$

$= 0.0305$

4. SP of A $= 20\%$ of $50 + ₹\ 50$

$= \dfrac{20}{100} \times 50 + 50$

$= 10 + 50 = ₹\ 60$

SP of B $= ₹\ 60 + 25\%$ of 60

$= 60 + \dfrac{25}{100} \times 60$

$= 60 + 15 = ₹\ 75$

SP of C $= 75 + 40\%$ of 75

$= 75 + \dfrac{40}{100} \times 75$

$= 75 + 30 = ₹\ 105$

Hence, the price D paid for the article $= ₹\ 105$

5. Let the required number $= x$

According to the question,

$$11 - x, \quad 15 - x, \quad 21 - x$$

$$(15 - x)^2 = (11 - x)(21 - x)$$

$\Rightarrow 225 + x^2 - 30x = 231 - 11x - 21x + x^2$

$\Rightarrow x^2 - 30x + 225 = x^2 - 32x + 231$

$\Rightarrow \qquad 2x = 6$

$\Rightarrow \qquad x = 3$

Hence, the required number $= 3$

6. $\qquad A = P\left(1+\dfrac{r}{100}\right)^t$

$\Rightarrow 3515.20 = P\left(1+\dfrac{r}{100}\right)^3 \qquad \ldots(i)$

and $\quad 3380 = P\left(1+\dfrac{r}{100}\right)^2 \qquad \ldots(ii)$

Dividing (i) by (ii)

$\dfrac{3515.20}{3380} = \left(1+\dfrac{r}{100}\right)$

$\Rightarrow 1+\dfrac{r}{100} = \dfrac{26}{25}$

$\Rightarrow \qquad \dfrac{r}{100} = \dfrac{26}{25} - 1 = \dfrac{1}{25}$

$\Rightarrow \qquad r = 4\%$

Putting the value of r in (ii)

$\Rightarrow \quad 3380 = P\left(1+\dfrac{4}{100}\right)^2$

$\Rightarrow \quad 3380 = P\left(\dfrac{26}{25} \times \dfrac{26}{25}\right)$

$\Rightarrow \qquad P = \dfrac{3380 \times 25 \times 25}{26 \times 26}$

$\Rightarrow \qquad P = 5 \times 625 = ₹\ 3125$

Hence, the money invested $= ₹\ 3125$

8. $\qquad$ Passed in English $= 77\%$

Passed in Mathematics $= 66\%$

Passed in both subjects = $(100 - 13) = 87\%$

Total passed $\% = 77 + 66 - 87 = 56\%$

$\therefore$ Total number of candidates

$$= \frac{100}{56} \times 392 = 700$$

10. $(1 + \cot\theta - \mathrm{cosec}\,\theta)(1 + \tan\theta + \sec\theta)$

$$= \left(1 + \frac{\cos\theta}{\sin\theta} - \frac{1}{\sin\theta}\right)\left(1 + \frac{\sin\theta}{\cos\theta} + \frac{1}{\cos\theta}\right)$$

$$= \left(\frac{\sin\theta + \cos\theta - 1}{\sin\theta}\right)\left(\frac{\cos\theta + \sin\theta + 1}{\cos\theta}\right)$$

$$= \frac{(\sin\theta + \cos\theta)^2 - (1)^2}{\sin\theta \cdot \cos\theta}$$

$$= \frac{\sin^2\theta + \cos^2\theta + 2\sin\theta \cdot \cos\theta - 1}{\sin\theta \cdot \cos\theta}$$

$$= \frac{1 + 2\sin\theta \cdot \cos\theta - 1}{\sin\theta \cdot \cos\theta} = \frac{2\sin\theta \cdot \cos\theta}{\sin\theta \cdot \cos\theta} = 2$$

11. $\sec 70° \cdot \sin 20° + \cos 20° \cdot \mathrm{cosec}\, 70°$

$= \sec(90° - 20°) \cdot \sin 20° + \cos 20°$

$\qquad\qquad\qquad\qquad \cdot \mathrm{cosec}(90° - 20°)$

$= \mathrm{cosec}\, 20° \cdot \sin 20° + \cos 20° \cdot \sec 20°$

$$= \frac{1}{\sin 20°} \times \sin 20° + \cos 20° \times \frac{1}{\cos 20°}$$

$= 1 + 1 = 2$

12. 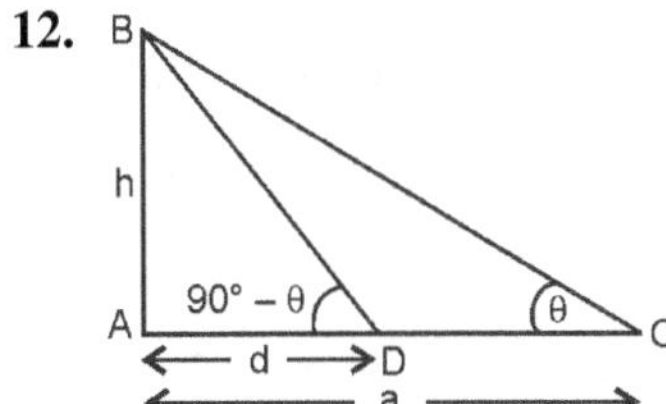

In $\triangle ABD$,

$$\tan(90° - \theta) = \frac{h}{b}$$

$$\cot\theta = \frac{h}{b} \qquad ...(i)$$

In $\triangle ABC$,

$$\tan\theta = \frac{h}{a} \qquad ...(ii)$$

Multiplying (i) and (ii)

$$\cot\theta \times \tan\theta = \frac{h}{b} \times \frac{h}{a} \Rightarrow 1 = \frac{h^2}{ab}$$

$$\Rightarrow \qquad h^2 = ab \Rightarrow h = \sqrt{ab}$$

Hence, the height of the tower $= \sqrt{ab}$

13. 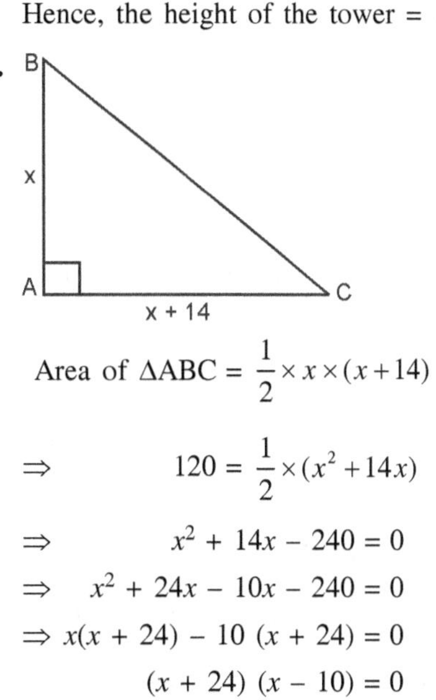

Area of $\triangle ABC = \dfrac{1}{2} \times x \times (x + 14)$

$$\Rightarrow \qquad 120 = \frac{1}{2} \times (x^2 + 14x)$$

$$\Rightarrow \qquad x^2 + 14x - 240 = 0$$

$$\Rightarrow \quad x^2 + 24x - 10x - 240 = 0$$

$$\Rightarrow x(x + 24) - 10(x + 24) = 0$$

$$(x + 24)(x - 10) = 0$$

either $x = -24$ or $x = 10$

but $x \neq -24$

$\therefore \qquad x = 10,$

$\qquad x + 14 = 10 + 14 = 24$

Now, $BC^2 = (10)^2 + (24)^2$

$$= 100 + 576 = 676$$

$\therefore \qquad BC = \sqrt{676} = 26$ cm

$\therefore$ Perimeter of $\triangle ABC = 10 + 24 + 26 = 60$ cm

14. Area of square $= x^2$

Area of circle $= \pi r^2$

$$\pi r^2 = x^2$$

$$\therefore \qquad r^2 = \frac{x^2}{\pi} \Rightarrow r = \frac{x}{\sqrt{\pi}}$$

$$\frac{2\pi r}{4x} = \frac{2\pi \times x}{4 \times x \times \sqrt{\pi}} = \frac{\sqrt{\pi}}{2}$$

$\therefore$ Required ratio $= \sqrt{\pi} : 2$

15.
$$\frac{V_1}{V_2} = \frac{\pi \times (2x)^2 \times 5x}{\pi(3x)^2 \times 3x} = \frac{4 \times 5}{9 \times 3} = \frac{20}{27}$$

$\therefore$ Required ratio = 20 : 27

16.

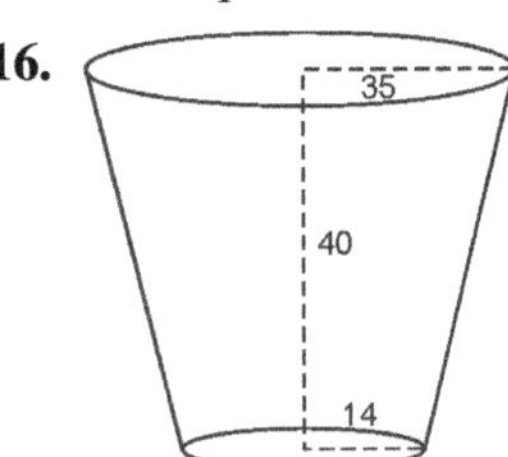

Volume of bucket

$$= \frac{1}{3} \times \pi(R^2 + r^2 + R \cdot r) \cdot h$$

$$= \frac{1}{3} \times \frac{22}{7}(35^2 + 14^2 + 35 \times 14) \times 40$$

$$= \frac{1}{3} \times \frac{22}{7}(1225 + 196 + 490) \times 40$$

$$= \frac{22}{21} \times 1911 \times 40$$

$$= 880 \times 91 = 80080 \text{ cm}^3$$

17. Mean $= 141 + 151 + 146 + 155 + 148 + 150 + 158$
$+ 147 + 159 + 152 + 153 + 149$

$$\frac{+150 + 160 + 161}{15}$$

$$= \frac{2280}{15} = 152$$

$\therefore$ Mean height = 152 cm

18. Total ball = 3 + 4 + 5 = 12

Required probability $= \dfrac{4}{12} = \dfrac{1}{3}$

24.   C l o c k is coded as
↓ ↓ ↓ ↓ ↓
3 6 9 3 8

L e a v e is coded as
↓ ↓ ↓ ↓ ↓
1 2 4 5 2

$\therefore$ C a v e is coded as
↓ ↓ ↓ ↓
3 4 5 2

25.   S   k   y   is coded as
↓   ↓   ↓
TT MM XX

$\therefore$ L i e is coded as
↓ ↓ ↓
MM KK DD

27. Let number of incorrect answers $= x$

$\therefore$ number of correct answers $= 180 - x$

According to the question,

$$(108 - x) \times 1 + (x)\left(-\frac{1}{3}\right) = 0$$

$$\Rightarrow \qquad 108 - x - \frac{x}{3} = 0$$

$$\Rightarrow \qquad x + \frac{x}{3} = 108$$

$$\Rightarrow \qquad \frac{4x}{3} = 108$$

$$\Rightarrow \qquad x = \frac{108 \times 3}{4} = 81$$

Hence, number of incorrect answers = 81

28. A has $(9 + 2 + 3 - 2) = 12$ marbles

29. B has $(9 - 2 + 2 - 3 + 2) = 13 - 5 = 8$ marbles

30. C has $(9 - 5 - 2) = 9 - 7 = 2$ marbles

31. D has $(9 + 2 - 1 - 3) = 11 - 4 = 7$ marbles

E has $(9 + 1 + 5 - 2 + 3) = 18 - 2 = 16$ marbles

Hence, E has got maximum no. of marbles.

32. 0   3   8   15   24   35   48
+3 +5 +7 +9 +11 +13

33. 2   9   30   93   282   849
2×3+3 9×3+3 30×3+3 93×3+3 282×3+3

34. 24   39   416   525   636   749
+109   +111   +113

35. 40   29   20   13   8
11   9   7   5

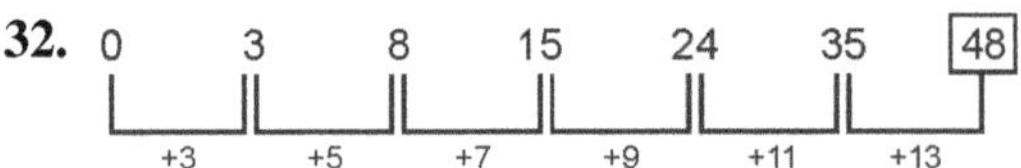

RRB—Railway Recruitment Board
Assistant Loco Pilot (ALP) & Technicians,
Recruitment Examination

FIRST STAGE COMPUTER BASED TEST (CBT)

1. The mean of reciprocal of x and y is equal to:
   A. $\dfrac{2(x+y)}{xy}$
   B. $\dfrac{x+y}{x-y}$
   C. $\dfrac{2x}{x+y}$
   D. $\dfrac{x+y}{2xy}$

2. The fractions given below are in their lowest terms. Supply the missing figures:
   $$5\dfrac{1}{x} \times y\dfrac{3}{4} = 20$$
   A. 3, 1
   B. 3, 3
   C. 1, 5
   D. 4, 1

3. Complete the series : 1, 2, 4, 7, 13, 24, 44, ?
   A. 80
   B. 64
   C. 81
   D. 66

4. Find the sum of all numbers up to 1000 which are divisible by 19.
   A. 26182
   B. 21588
   C. 13262
   D. 33868

5. The average of three numbers is 135. The largest number is 180 and the difference of other two is 25. The smallest number is:
   A. 130
   B. 100
   C. 125
   D. 120

6. Ten per cent of twenty plus twenty per cent of ten equals:
   A. 2 per cent of 200
   B. 1 per cent of 200
   C. 10 per cent of 20
   D. 20 per cent of 10

7. If 70% of P is equal to 40% of Q. The ratio of P to Q is:
   A. 4 : 7
   B. 7 : 4
   C. 4 : 11
   D. 7 : 11

8. If a clock strikes 12 times in 22 seconds. In how much time it will strike 6 times?
   A. 10 seconds
   B. 11 seconds
   C. 15 seconds
   D. 8 seconds

9. HCF of two numbers is 24 and LCM is 5304. If one of the number is 408, then other number is:
   A. 1146
   B. 312
   C. 32
   D. 302

10. Sohan is three times older than Gopal. Five years back, he was four times older than Gopal. Find the present age of Gopal.
    A. 15 years
    B. 18 years
    C. 20 years
    D. 12 years

11. If all the triangles on the same base and within the same parallels, the perimeter is least if the triangle is:
    A. Equilateral
    B. Isosceles
    C. Right angled
    D. Obtuse angled

12. $\tan 30° \cos 60° \sin 60° = ?$
    A. $\dfrac{1}{\sqrt{3}}$
    B. $\dfrac{1}{2}$
    C. 1
    D. $\dfrac{1}{4}$

13. The value of $\dfrac{\sin 39°}{\cos 51°}$ is:
    A. 0
    B. $\dfrac{1}{2}$
    C. ∞
    D. 1

14. 70% of 280 is same as:
    A. 40% of 49
    B. 35% of 140
    C. 7% of 28
    D. None of these

15. The average of 7 consecutive numbers is 33. The highest of these numbers is:
A. 30
B. 33
C. 36
D. 35

16. What is the number in the series in place of the question mark?

    0, 2, 6, ?, 30, 62
A. 18
B. 24
C. 14
D. 10

17. Find the value of $5\dfrac{6}{7} \times 3\dfrac{1}{4} + 40\%$ of $35 = ?$

A. $17\dfrac{17}{28}$
B. $16\dfrac{17}{28}$

C. $16\dfrac{9}{14}$
D. $33\dfrac{1}{28}$

18. Which of the following values are equal?
(*i*) 1^4
(*ii*) 4^0
(*iii*) 0^4
(*iv*) 4^1
A. (*i*) and (*iv*)
B. (*i*) and (*iii*)
C. (*i*) and (*ii*)
D. (*ii*) and (*iii*)

19. Which of the following would be the next number in the series 8, 15, 29, 57?
A. 99
B. 113
C. 103
D. 101

20. Which of the following numbers will be inserted in place of the (?) mark?

35 (78) 40   45 (97) 35   25 (?) 30
A. 66
B. 56
C. 67
D. 71

21. Find the missing term in the following:
ACEG : DFHJ : : QSUV : ?
A. TVXY
B. MNPR
C. OQST
D. KMNP

22. Find the odd man out from the following words:
A. Gun
B. Rifle
C. Sabers
D. Revolver

23. Find the odd man out.
A. Glaucoma
B. Cataract
C. Eczema
D. Trachoma

24. Which of the following number will be placed in place of the (?) mark in the number series?
3, 5, 6, ? , 9, 15
A. 10
B. 12
C. 15
D. 22

25. If 'BEARING' is coded as 1234567. 'PARE' will be coded as:
A. 4234
B. 4321
C. 4345
D. 4342

26. If RADIO is coded as 'UDGLR', PHOTO will be coded as:
A. OIPWR
B. OTOPT
C. SKRWR
D. SKPWR

27. 10 women can harvest a field in 3 days. How many women can harvest the same field in 2 days?
A. 29
B. 15
C. 30
D. 35

28. In an examination, 360 students passed out of 450. Find the percentage of pass students.
A. 80%
B. 60%
C. 20%
D. 70%

29. What percentage of 85 is 17?
A. 25%
B. 30%
C. 5%
D. 20%

30. If the price of sugar is 25% more than price of Gur, then price of Gur is how much per cent less than sugar?
A. 25%
B. 20%
C. 80%
D. 30%

31. A truck covers a distance of 51 km in 8.5 litres of diesel. How much diesel is required to cover a distance of 165 km?
A. 27.5 litres
B. 2.5 litres
C. 30 litres
D. 21.5 litres

32. If $23 : 23 : : 23 : x$. Then value of x is:
A. 23
B. 47
C. 69
D. 70

33. If 'friend' bears relation to 'friendly' which word in the options given below bear the same relation with opponent?
A. Enemy
B. Hostile
C. Defeat
D. Contest

34. The cost of 16 cm of cloth is ₹ 60, calculate the cost of 6 cm.
   A. ₹ 22.5   B. ₹ 26
   C. ₹ 56   D. ₹ 62

35. The difference between 20% of 172 and 272 is:
   A. 40   B. 20
   C. 35   D. 30

36. Find the largest number which can divide 124 and 93 exactly.
   A. 24   B. 31
   C. 26   D. 27

37. Which of the following represents a chemical change?
   A. Evaporation of alcohol
   B. Sublimation of iodine
   C. Heating of a platinum wire in a bunsen flame
   D. Heating of mercuric oxide powder

38. The chemical used as a 'fixer' in photography is:
   A. Sodium sulphate
   B. Sodium thiosulphate
   C. Ammonium persulphate
   D. Borax

39. Which of the following in solid state is known as dry ice?
   A. Ammonia   B. Nitrogen
   C. Carbon dioxide   D. Hydrogen

40. The tape of tape recorder is coated with:
   A. Copper sulphate
   B. Mercury
   C. Ferromagnetic powder
   D. Zinc oxide

41. During dehydration, what is slightly lost actually?
   A. Sodium Chloride   B. Potassium Chloride
   C. Calcium Chloride   D. Calcium Sulphate

42. Rayon is chemically a:
   A. cellulose   B. amylase
   C. glucose   D. pectin

43. The process of obtaining salt from sea water is called:
   A. Evaporation   B. Sublimation
   C. Crystallization   D. Distillation

44. The silver surface of thermos flask prevents the transfer of heat by:
   A. Convection   B. Conduction
   C. Radiation   D. Reflection

45. The hardness of water can be removed by:
   A. Zeeolite   B. Sodium Silicate
   C. Boiling   D. None of these

46. The most common acid found in the nature is:
   A. Citric acid   B. Lactic acid
   C. Acetic acid   D. Hydrochloric acid

47. The speed of light will be minimum, while passing through:
   A. Vacuum   B. Glass
   C. Air   D. Water

48. The final image produced by a simple microscope is:
   A. Virtual and erect   B. Erect and real
   C. Real and inverted   D. Virtual and real

49. The change of ice into water is a/an:
   A. Chemical change   B. Physical change
   C. Atomic change   D. Electrical change

50. An air bubble in water will act like a:
   A. Convex lens   B. Convex mirror
   C. Concave lens   D. Concave mirror

51. Plants absorb water from the soil by:
   A. Gravitational process
   B. Capillary process
   C. Hygroscopic process
   D. None of these

52. The main endocrine gland present in human body is:
   A. Pituitary gland   B. Adrenal gland
   C. Thyroid gland   D. Pancreas gland

53. In human body, the water quantity is about:
   A. 20%   B. 100%
   C. 80%   D. 65%

54. Which of the following chemicals is used for preserving fruit juices in India?
   A. Sodium hydroxide
   B. Potassium nitrate
   C. Ammonium sulphate
   D. Sodium benzoate

55. Mohen-jo-daro is situated at:
   A. Punjab B. Gujarat
   C. Sindh D. Uttar Pradesh

56. The first governor general of the independent India was:
   A. C. Rajagopalachari
   B. Dr. Rajendra Prasad
   C. Lord Mountbatten
   D. Dr. B.R. Ambedkar

57. Grand Trunk road was made by:
   A. Chandragupta Maurya
   B. Shahjahan
   C. Shershah Suri
   D. Lord Dalhousi

58. Large production of jute is at the delta of river:
   A. Damodar B. Sindh
   C. Ganga D. Satluj

59. Which state of India is largest in area?
   A. Uttar Pradesh B. Madhya Pradesh
   C. Assam D. West Bengal

60. The highest mountain peak in India is:
   A. Kanchenjunga B. Mount Everest
   C. Nanda Devi D. Annapurna

61. Largest river in India is:
   A. Ganga B. Kaveri
   C. Brahmaputra D. Godavari

62. Father of local self governance is:
   A. Lord Ripen B. Lord Curzon
   C. Lord Minto D. Lord Dalhousi

63. Section 370 of Constitution of India gives special status to which state?
   A. Sikkim
   B. Nagaland
   C. Arunachal Pradesh
   D. Jammu and Kashmir

64. The members of Rajya Sabha are elected:
   A. Directly by people
   B. By members of parliament
   C. By members of legislative assembly
   D. By the President of India

65. Who constitutes the Finance Commission?
   A. Lok Sabha B. President
   C. Rajya Sabha D. Finance Minister

66. Who is the Chairperson of Planning Commission?
   A. Prime Minister B. Home Minister
   C. President D. Finance Minister

67. Panchayati Raj system was first introduced in the state of:
   A. Bihar B. West Bengal
   C. Andhra Pradesh D. Rajasthan

68. The capital of Sikkim is:
   A. Gangtok B. Shillong
   C. Imphal D. Dispur

69. The state with highest population density is:
   A. Uttar Pradesh B. Arunachal Pradesh
   C. West Bengal D. Bihar

70. The smallest state of India is:
   A. Haryana B. Punjab
   C. Bihar D. Goa

71. The state with highest number of tribes is:
   A. West Bengal B. Bihar
   C. Jharkhand D. Madhya Pradesh

72. Who said 'Go back to Vedas'?
   A. Dayanand Saraswati
   B. Vivekananda
   C. Swami Shradhananda
   D. Ram Krishna Paramhansa

73. When Alexander invaded India, who were the ruler of Magadh:
   A. Shishunagas B. Nandas
   C. Mauryas D. None of these

74. Which of the following may be used by the Reserve Bank of India as a tool to draining out excess money from the system:
   A. Increasing Cash Reserve Ratio
   B. Increasing Reverse Repo rate
   C. Reduction in Repo rate
   D. Both (A) & (B)

75. Mullaperiyar dam is in the state of .... and there is a interstate dispute between .... for this.
   A. Kerala, Kerala and Tamilnadu
   B. Kerala, Kerala and Karnataka
   C. Karnataka, Karnataka and Kerala
   D. Tamilnadu, Tamilnadu and Kerala

ANSWERS

1	2	3	4	5	6	7	8	9	10
D	B	C	A	B	A	A	A	B	A

11	12	13	14	15	16	17	18	19	20
D	D	D	D	C	C	D	C	B	B

21	22	23	24	25	26	27	28	29	30
A	C	C	A	D	C	B	A	D	B

31	32	33	34	35	36	37	38	39	40
A	A	B	A	B	B	D	B	C	C

41	42	43	44	45	46	47	48	49	50
A	A	A	B	C	A	A	D	B	C

51	52	53	54	55	56	57	58	59	60
B	D	D	D	C	C	C	C	B	A

61	62	63	64	65	66	67	68	69	70
A	A	D	C	B	A	D	A	D	D

71	72	73	74	75
D	A	B	D	A

EXPLANATORY ANSWERS

1. Reciprocal of $x = \dfrac{1}{x}$

and reciprocal of $y = \dfrac{1}{y}$

$$\text{Mean} = \frac{\dfrac{1}{x} + \dfrac{1}{y}}{2} = \frac{\dfrac{y+x}{xy}}{2}$$

$$= \frac{x+y}{2xy}.$$

2. $5\dfrac{1}{x} \times y\dfrac{3}{4} = 20$

$\Rightarrow \quad \dfrac{5x+1}{x} \times \dfrac{4y+3}{4} = 20$

$\Rightarrow \quad (5x+1)(4y+3) = 80x$

By putting $x = y = 3$ we get the required result.

Hence, $\quad x = 3$

$\quad y = 3.$

3. 1, 2, 4, 7, 13, 24, 44, ?

$$1 + 2 + 4 = 7$$
$$2 + 4 + 7 = 13$$
$$4 + 7 + 13 = 24$$
$$7 + 13 + 24 = 44$$
$$13 + 24 + 44 = 81$$

Hence, next number is 81.

4. 19, 38, 57, ... 988

$$988 = a + (n-1)d$$
$$= 19 + (n-1)19$$
$$= 19 + 19n - 19$$

$\Rightarrow \quad 19n = 988$

$\Rightarrow \quad n = 52$

$$S_{52} = \frac{52}{2}\{2 \times 19 + (52-1)19\}$$
$$= 26\{38 + 51 \times 19\}$$
$$= 26\{38 + 969\}$$
$$= 26 \times 1007 = 26182$$

5. Let numbers are A, B and C.

$$A + B + C = 135 \times 3 = 405$$

Let C = 180

$$\therefore \qquad A + B = 405 - 180 = 225$$

$$B - A = 25$$

$$\therefore \qquad 2B = 225 + 25 = 250$$

$$B = 125$$

$$A + B = 225$$

$$\Rightarrow \qquad A = 225 - 125 = 100$$

$\therefore$ Smallest number = 100.

6. 10% of 20 + 20% of 10

$$= \frac{10}{100} \times 20 + \frac{20}{100} \times 10$$

$$= 2 + 2 = 4$$

$$2\% \text{ of } 200 = \frac{2}{100} \times 200 = 4$$

7. 70% of P = 40% of Q

$$\Rightarrow \qquad \frac{70}{100} \times P = \frac{40}{100} \times Q$$

$$\frac{7P}{10} = \frac{4Q}{10}$$

$$\Rightarrow \qquad 7P = 4Q$$

$$\Rightarrow \qquad \frac{P}{Q} = \frac{4}{7}$$

Hence, ratio of P : Q = 4 : 7.

8. In order to hear 12 strikes, there are 11 intervals (12 − 1) and time of each interval is uniform.

Hence, time to hear each strike is 22 ÷ 11

$$= 2 \text{ seconds.}$$

Now to hear 6 strikes, there are (6 − 1) *i.e.*, 5 intervals for which the time taken is 5 × 2

$$= 10 \text{ seconds.}$$

Hence, it will take 10 seconds for a clock to strike 6.

9.

$$\text{Other number} = \frac{\text{HCF} \times \text{LCM}}{\text{One number}}$$

$$= \frac{24 \times 5304}{408} = 312.$$

10. Let present age of Gopal be x years

$$\therefore \qquad \text{Sohan's age} = 3x \text{ years}$$

5 years ago, Gopal's age = $(x - 5)$ years

5 years ago, Sohan's age = $(3x - 5)$ years

According to the question,

$$3x - 5 = 4(x - 5)$$

$$\Rightarrow \qquad 3x - 5 = 4x - 20$$

$$\Rightarrow \qquad x = 15$$

Hence, Gopal's present age = 15 years.

12. tan 30° × cos 60° × sin 60°

$$= \frac{1}{\sqrt{3}} \times \frac{1}{2} \times \frac{\sqrt{3}}{2} = \frac{1}{4}.$$

13. $\dfrac{\sin 39°}{\cos 51°} = \dfrac{\sin 39°}{\cos(90 - 39°)} = \dfrac{\sin 39°}{\sin 39°} = 1.$

14.

$$70\% \text{ of } 280 = \frac{70}{100} \times 280 = 196$$

$$40\% \text{ of } 49 = \frac{40}{100} \times 49 \neq 196$$

$$35\% \text{ of } 140 = \frac{35}{100} \times 140 = 49 \neq 196$$

$$7\% \text{ of } 28 = \frac{7}{100} \times 28 = \frac{196}{100} \neq 196$$

Hence, correct answer is D.

15. $x + (x + 1) + (x + 2) + (x + 3) + (x + 4) + (x + 5) + (x + 6) = 33 \times 7$

$$7x + 21 = 231$$

$$\Rightarrow \qquad 7x = 210$$

$$\Rightarrow \qquad x = 30$$

$\therefore$ The highest number

$$= x + 6 = 30 + 6 = 36.$$

16.

0,	2,	6,	?,	30,	62
↓	↓	↓	↓	↓	↓
0×2+2	2×2+2	6×2+2	14×2+2	30×2+2	

Hence, the number in place of question mark = 14.

17. $5\dfrac{6}{7} \times 3\dfrac{1}{4} + 40\% \text{ of } 35$

$$= \frac{41}{7} \times \frac{13}{4} + \frac{40}{100} \times 35$$

$$= \frac{533}{28} + 14 = \frac{533 + 392}{28}$$

$$= \frac{925}{28} = 33\frac{1}{28}.$$

18. $1^4 = 1 \times 1 \times 1 \times 1 = 1$

$4^0 = 1$ 　　　　　　　$(\because x^0 = 1)$

Hence, both are equal.

19. 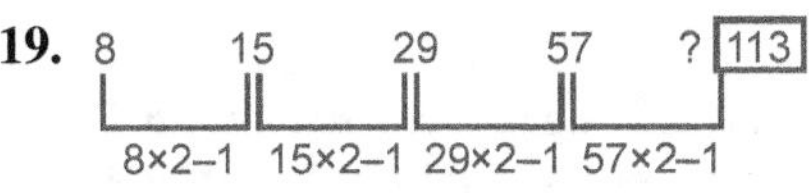

Hence, required number = 113.

21. 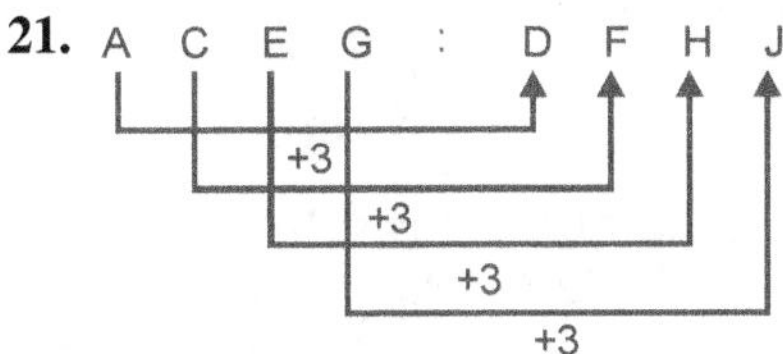

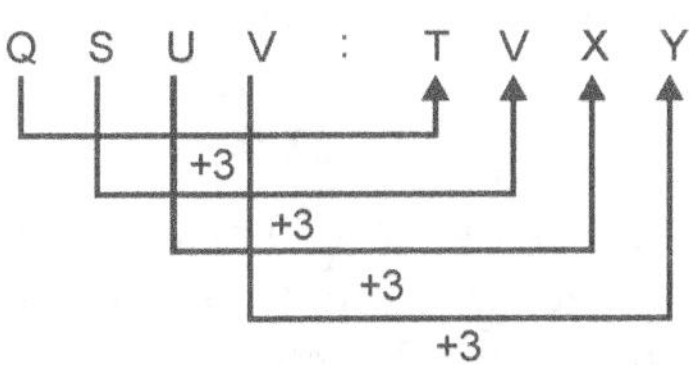

22. Gun, rifle and revolver are weapons used for firing bullets whereas saber is a heavy sword with curved blade used in the sport of fencing.

23. Glaucoma, cataract and trachoma are diseases related to eye whereas eczema is a medical condition in which patches of skin become rough.

24.

Hence, number 10 will be placed in place of the (?) mark in the number series.

25.
```
B  E  A  R  I  N  G      R  A  R  E
↓  ↓  ↓  ↓  ↓  ↓  ↓      ↓  ↓  ↓  ↓
1  2  3  4  5  6  7      4  3  4  2
```

27. No. of women harvest the field in 3 days = 10

In 2 days $= \dfrac{10 \times 3}{2} = 15$ women

Hence, required number of women = 15

28. Out of 450 students 360 students passed.

Required percentage $= \dfrac{360}{450} \times 100 = 80\%$

29. $x\%$ of $85 = 17$

$\Rightarrow \dfrac{x}{100} \times 85 = 17 \quad \Rightarrow x = \dfrac{17 \times 100}{85} = 20\%$

Hence, 20% of 85 = 17.

30. Required percentage $= \left(\dfrac{25}{100 + 25} \times 100 \right)$

$$= \dfrac{25}{125} \times 100 = 20\%$$

31. 51 km distance covers in 8.5 litres of diesel.

165 km distance covers in $\dfrac{8.5}{51} \times 165$ litrees

$$= .5 \times 55 = 27.5 \text{ litres}$$

32. $\dfrac{23}{23} = \dfrac{23}{x}$

$\Rightarrow 1 = \dfrac{23}{x} \qquad \Rightarrow x = 23.$

33. As friend behaves in a kind or friendly way. Opponent behaves in unfriendly or hostile way.

34. Cost of 16 cm of cloth = ₹ 60

Cost of 6 cm of cloth $= ₹\ \dfrac{60}{16} \times 6 = ₹\ 22.5.$

35. $(272 - 172)$ of $20\% = 100 \times \dfrac{20}{100} = 20.$

36. HCF of 124 and 93 = 31

Hence, largest number = 31.

RRB—Railway Recruitment Board
Assistant Loco Pilot (ALP) & Technicians,
Recruitment Examination

FIRST STAGE COMPUTER BASED TEST (CBT)

1. The value of $\dfrac{1}{1+\sqrt{2}}+\dfrac{1}{\sqrt{2}+\sqrt{3}}+\dfrac{1}{\sqrt{3}+\sqrt{4}}$

   $+..........+\dfrac{1}{\sqrt{8}+\sqrt{9}}$ is :

   A. 1   B. –1
   C. 2   D. –2

2. The smallest number which is a perfect square and contains 7936 as a factor is :
   A. 264016
   B. 241606
   C. 246160
   D. 246016

3. The value of

   $\left(\dfrac{1}{x^{a-b}}\right)^{\frac{1}{a-c}} \times \left(\dfrac{1}{x^{b-c}}\right)^{\frac{1}{b-a}} \times \left(\dfrac{1}{x^{c-a}}\right)^{\frac{1}{c-b}}$ is—

   A. 0   B. –1
   C. 1   D. 2

4. A sum of ₹ 1200 is lent partly at 6% and partly at 4%. If the total interest for $3\dfrac{1}{2}$ years be ₹ 224, the amount lent at 6% is—
   A. ₹ 800
   B. ₹ 252
   C. ₹ 224
   D. ₹ 168

5. A's share is to B's share as 3 : 4 and B's share is to C's share as 6 : 7. The ratio of the shares of A to C is—
   A. 12 : 14   B. 9 : 12
   C. 9 : 14   D. 4 : 6

6. The price of sugar increased by 25%. How much per cent should a man decrease his consumption so that there is no increase in his expenditure ?
   A. 25%   B. 20%
   C. 15%   D. 10%

7. The list price of a pen is ₹ 160. A customer buys it for ₹ 122.40. He gets two successive discounts - one 10% and the other unknown. The rate of second discount is—
   A. 4%   B. 15%
   C. 6%   D. 8%

8. A man sells a toy for ₹ 80 more than he paid for it and realizes a profit equal to two-fifths of its cost price. The cost price of the toy is—
   A. ₹ 300   B. ₹ 250
   C. ₹ 225   D. ₹ 200

9. A train takes half an hour more to do a journey when it is running at 25 km an hour than when it is running 30 km an hour. The length of the journey is—
   A. 200 km   B. 150 km
   C. 100 km   D. 75 km

10. The value of

    $\left(\dfrac{\sin 27^\circ}{\cos 63^\circ}\right)^{2}+\left(\dfrac{\cos 63^\circ}{\cos 27^\circ}\right)^{2} - 2\sin 30^\circ$ is :

    A. 2   B. –2
    C. 1   D. –1

11. The value of 0 less than 90° which satisfy the equation $3\tan\theta + \cot\theta = 5\csc\theta$ is :
    A. 30°   B. 45°
    C. 60°   D. 15°

12. From the top of a building 60 metres high the angles of depression of the top and bottom of a tower are observed to be 30° and 60°. The height of the tower is :

    A. 40 m   B. $40\sqrt{3}$ m

    C. 20 m   D. $20\sqrt{3}$ m

13. The ages of 12 persons are given below :
48, 42, 47, 43, 48, 56, 50, 56, 65, 56, 65, 60
The modal age is :
    A. 65   B. 56
    C. 50   D. 60

14. A room 5 m long and 4 m wide is surrounded by a Verandah which occupies 22 sq m. The width of the Verandah is :
    A. 1 m   B. 1.5 m
    C. 2 m   D. 2.5 m

15. A cone and a cylinder are of the same height. Their radii of the bases are in the ratio of 2 : 1. The ratio of their volumes is :
    A. 2 : 3   B. 3 : 2
    C. 3 : 4   D. 4 : 3

16. A right circular cone is 8 cm high and the radius of the base is 2 cm. The cone is melted and recast into a sphere. The diameter of the sphere is:
    A. 8 cm   B. 6 cm
    C. 4 cm   D. 2 cm

17. The mean of the following data is 20.6.
x : 10   15   20   25   35
f : 3   10 x 7   5
The missing frequency (x) is
    A. 25
    B. 15
    C. 10
    D. 8

18. If two coins are tossed once, the probability of getting at least one head is :

    A. $\dfrac{1}{2}$ B. $\dfrac{1}{4}$

    C. $\dfrac{2}{3}$ D. $\dfrac{3}{4}$

Direction (*Q. 19-22*): *Each of the following two statements are followed by two conclusions. Assuming that the given statements are true, you have to decide which conclusion follows strictly from the given statements. Select your answer from the alternatives.*

19. Statement:
All boys are not students.
Some students are not employed.
Conclusions :
I. These boys are not employed.
II. Some employed one are not boys.
    A. Only I follows
    B. Only II follows
    C. Both I and II follow
    D. Neither I nor II follows

20. Statements:
All furnitures are pens.
All pens are pencils.
Conclusions :
I. Some furnitures are pencils.
II. All pencils are furnitures.
    A. Only I follows
    B. Only II follows
    C. Both I and II follow
    D. Neither I nor II follows

21. Statements:
No dog is animal.
No animal is living being.
Conclusions:
I. No animal is dog.
II. Some living beings are dogs.
    A. Only I follows
    B. Only II follows
    C. Both I and II follow
    D. Neither I nor II follows

22. Statements:
No bird has wings.
All birds are rational.
Conclusions :
I. Wingless beings are birds.
II. Some rationals are birds.
    A. Only I follows
    B. Only II follows
    C. Both I and II follow
    D. Neither I nor II follows

Direction (Q. 23-26): *In the following questions a series is being given. Select from the alternatives the correct term to fill in the missing term.*

23. 5, 7, 10, 11, 15, 15, 20,.........
  A. 22   B. 19
  C. 20   D. 21

24. $\dfrac{2}{\sqrt{5}}, \dfrac{3}{5}, \dfrac{4}{5\sqrt{5}}, \dfrac{5}{25}$,.......

  A. $\dfrac{6}{25}$ B. $\dfrac{7}{25}$

  C. $\dfrac{6}{25\sqrt{5}}$ D. $\dfrac{7}{25\sqrt{5}}$

25. 3, 15, 39, 75,......,
  A. 93   B. 101
  C. 99   D. 123

26. 25, 25, 27, 22, 30, 19, 34, 16,.......
  A. 39   B. 35
  C. 32   D. 13

Directions (Q. 27-30): *The following questions are based on the following diagrams. Circles (irrespectives of the size or location) represent objects. You have to identify which of the following diagrams would represent best the relationship between given terms.*

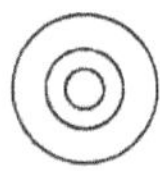 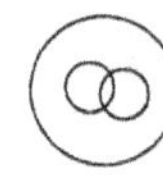  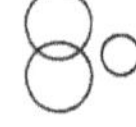 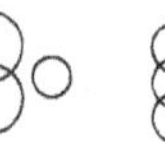
  (a)   (b)   (c)   (d)   (e)

27. Which of the above five diagrams would best represent - Musicians, Instrumentalists, Violinists?
  A. (a)   B. (b)
  C. (c)   D. (e)

28. Which of the above five diagrams would best represent - People, Painters, Boys?
  A. (e)   B. (d)
  C. (a)   D. (b)

29. Which of the above five diagrams would best represent - Mothers, Fathers and Teachers?
  A. (a)   B. (b)
  C. (d)   D. (e)

30. Which of the above five diagrams would best represent - Men, Women and Children?
  A. (a)
  B. (c)
  C. (e)
  D. None

Direction (Q. 31-34): *In the following questions, there are two sets of figures. You have to find a figure from the answer figures which can best suit the question figure series.*

31. Problem Figure

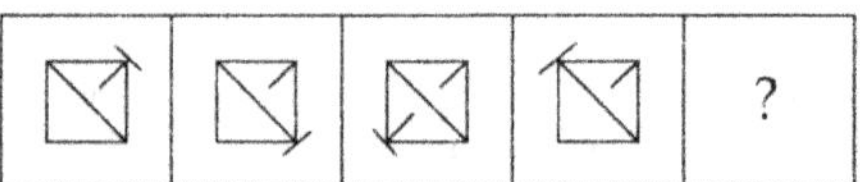

Answer Figures

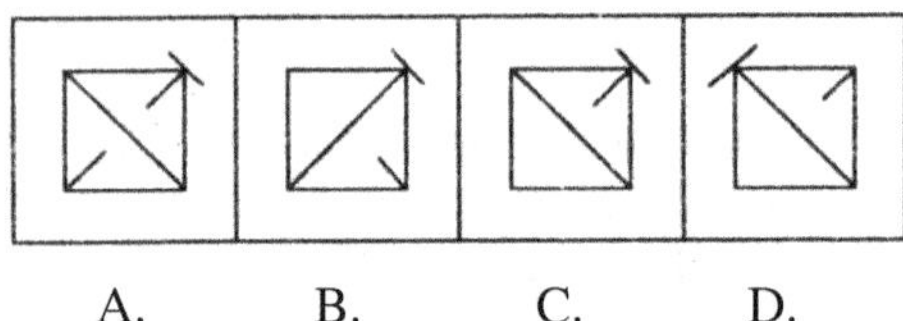
  A.   B.   C.   D.

32. Problem Figure

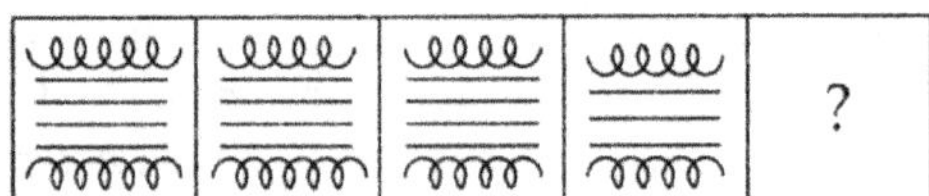

Answer Figures

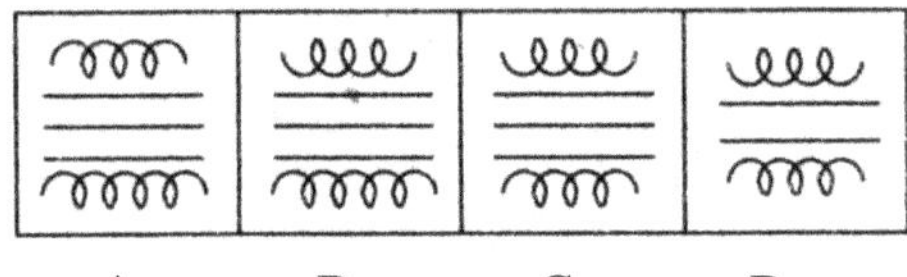
  A.   B.   C.   D.

33. Problem Figure

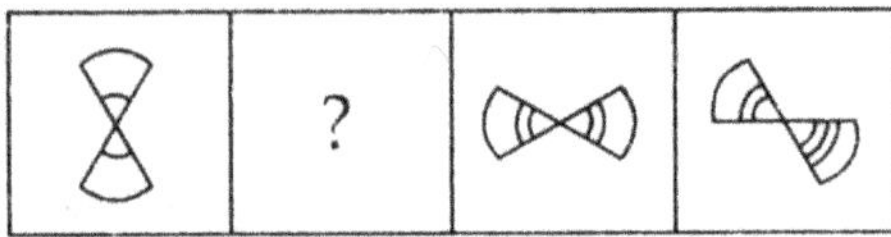

Answer Figures

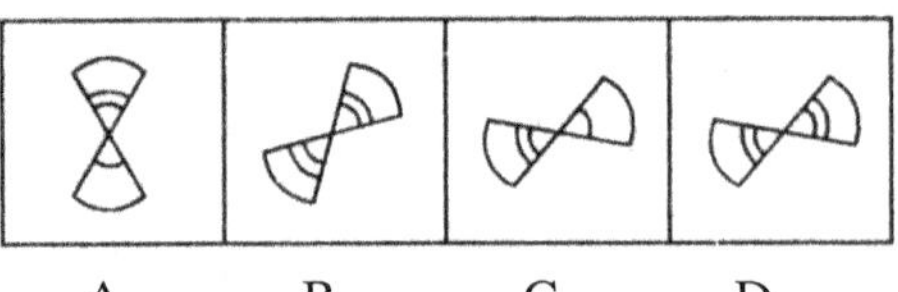
  A.   B.   C.   D.

34. Problem Figure

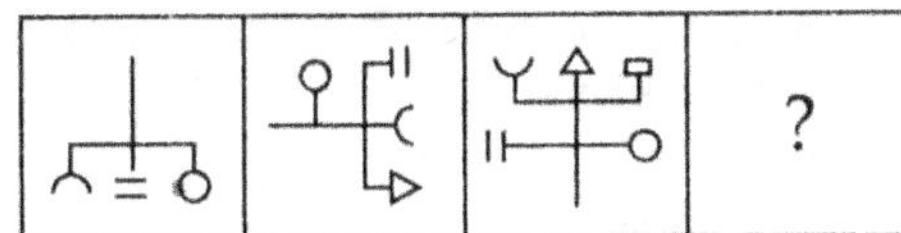

Answer Figures

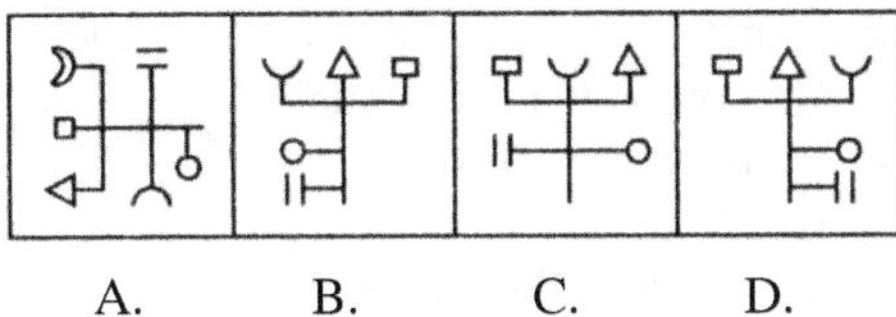

    A.   B.   C.   D.

35. A student gets one mark for every correct answer but 1/3 mark is deducted for every wrong answer he gives. In 108 questions his total score is zero. How many questions has he answered wrong?
A. 27
B. 30
C. 81
D. 54

36. Identify the odd member of this group?
A. 13
B. 61
C. 73
D. 69

37. Refractive index of a medium—
A. has no unit
B. has an unit
C. has a value equal to 1 or less than one
D. has a value less than one

38. Three primary colours are—
A. red, green and yellow
B. red, green and blue
C. green, yellow and orange
D. violet, yellow and red

39. Which physical quantity is represented by Coulomb per second?
A. charge
B. electric current
C. potential difference
D. resistance

40. A wire of resistance 2 ohms is bent in the form of a closed circle. The effective resistance between the two points at the end of any diameter of the circle is:
A. 0.5 ohm
B. 1 ohm
C. 2 ohms
D. 4 ohms

41. The frequency of an alternating current whose direction changes after every 0.01 second is:
A. 1 Hz
B. 2 Hz
C. 50 Hz
D. 100 Hz

42. How much solar energy will be received by 1 m^2 area in one hour? (Solar constant = 1.4 kW/m^2)—
A. 1400 × 1 J
B. 1400 × 60 J
C. 1.40 × 60 × 60 J
D. 1400 × 60 × 60 J

43. Speed of light is maximum in the following (out of 4 given media)—
A. water
B. glass
C. diamond
D. air

44. Average age of red blood cells (RBC) is approximately:
A. one day
B. 30 days
C. 60 days
D. 120 days

45. On adding lime juice to distilled water its pH—
A. remains unchanged
B. becomes 7
C. becomes less than 7
D. becomes more than 7

46. The valency shown by an element having atomic number 12 is—
A. 1
B. 2
C. 4
D. 6

47. Chemical formula for baking soda is—
A. $NaOH$
B. $NaHCO_3$
C. $Ca(OH)_2$
D. Na_2CO_3

48. Pure gold is :
A. 1 carat gold
B. 18 carat gold
C. 22 carat gold
D. 24 carat gold

49. The agency responsible for running space research programmes in India is—
A. IRS
B. UGC
C. ISRO
D. IARI

50. The first Indian satellite sent to space was named—
A. Rohini
B. Dhruv
C. Aryabhatt
D. Sputnik

51. In Hydrilla plant stomata are present—
A. On stem
B. On leaves
C. On both stem and leaves
D. No where as they are absent in Hydrilla

52. The excretory unit of kidney is—
A. neuron
B. hormone
C. photon
D. nephron

53. The author of the book 'The origin of species' is—
A. Charles Darwin
B. Lamarck
C. J.D. Watson
D. Weismann

54. The time period of geosynchronous satellite is—
A. One hour
B. Twelve hours
C. Twenty-four hours
D. One year

55. The most important kingdom in Deccan and Central India after the Maurya has that of the :
A. Satvahans
B. Cholas
C. Pallavas
D. Pandyan

56. Alberuni came to India in:
A. 9th Century AD
B. 10th Century AD
C. 11th Century AD
D. 12th Century AD

57. The planning commission was set up in:
A. March 1950
B. March 1951
C. April 1951
D. April 1952

58. What is the consequence of the writ of Habeas Corpus?
A. The person under detention is set free
B. The public servant is restrained from taking any action
C. The officer not competent to take certain action is told not to go ahead with the action
D. More information is sought from the lower court

59. Which of the following river is called 'Biological Desert' due to heavy population?
A. Brahmaputra
B. Ganga
C. Damodar
D. Yamuna

60. Which of the following foreign kings was not a contemporary of Ashoka?
A. Antiochos Theos
B. Magas
C. Ptolemy Philadelphos
D. Daurius II

61. Who is remembered as the pioneer of Economic Nationalism?
A. Bipin Chandar Pal
B. Gokhale
C. R.C. Dutt
D. Madan Mohan Malviya

62. Lapps inhabit—
A. East Africa
B. European Steppes
C. South American grasslands
D. European Tundra

63. India's national game is :
A. Football
B. Cricket
C. Tennis
D. Hockey

64. Who is one of the propounders of the binary star theories?
A. Laplace
B. Kant
C. La-Pichon
D. Jeffreys

65. In which state was Panchayat Raj first introduced?
A. Gujarat
B. Rajasthan
C. Bihar
D. Andhra Pradesh

66. The electoral system of India is largely based on the pattern of :
A. Britain
B. France
C. USA
D. None of these

67. Monoculture is a typical characteristic of :
A. Shifting cultivation
B. Subsistence farming
C. Specialized horticulture
D. Commercial grain farming

68. Horse latitudes is the term applied to the :
A. 0° – 5° N and S latitudes
B. Polar circles
C. 30° – 40° N and S latitudes
D. 40° – 60° N and S latitudes

69. In the vedic period goghna refers to :
A. One who gifts cattle
B. One who slaughters cattle
C. A guest
D. The bridegroom

70. 'Half an hour discussion' can be raised in the house of parliament after giving notice to the :
A. Presiding officer of the house
B. The Secretary-General of the house
C. The Secretary of the department of parliamentary affairs
D. Concerned minister

71. Fiscal policy is connected with :
A. Exports and imports
B. Public revenue and Expenditure
C. Issue of currency
D. Population control

72. Who of the following was the first speaker of Lok Sabha?
A. Hukum Singh
B. G.S. Dhilon
C. G.V. Mavalankar
D. Ananthaswayanam Ayenger

73. A LAN card is also known as a:
A. ASIC
B. BUS
C. NIC
D. MMX

74. A UPS:
A. Increases the storage capacity of a computer system
B. Increases the process speed
C. Provides backup power in the event of a power cut
D. None of these

75. A group of 4 bits is called:
A. Byte
B. Nibble
C. Word
D. None of these

ANSWERS

1	2	3	4	5	6	7	8	9	10
C	D	C	A	C	B	B	D	D	C

11	12	13	14	15	16	17	18	19	20
C	A	B	A	D	C	A	D	B	A

21	22	23	24	25	26	27	28	29	30
A	B	C	C	D	A	A	D	D	D

31	32	33	34	35	36	37	38	39	40
C	B	A	A	C	D	C	B	A	B

41	42	43	44	45	46	47	48	49	50
C	C	D	D	C	B	B	D	C	C

51	52	53	54	55	56	57	58	59	60
D	D	A	C	A	C	A	A	D	D

61	62	63	64	65	66	67	68	69	70
C	D	D	B	B	A	B	C	C	B

71	72	73	74	75
B	C	C	C	B

EXPLANATORY ANSWERS

1. $\dfrac{1}{1+\sqrt{2}} \times \dfrac{\sqrt{2}-1}{\sqrt{2}-1} = \dfrac{\sqrt{2}-1}{2-1} = \sqrt{2}-1$

$\dfrac{1}{\sqrt{3}+\sqrt{2}} \times \dfrac{\sqrt{3}-\sqrt{2}}{\sqrt{3}-\sqrt{2}} = \dfrac{\sqrt{3}-\sqrt{2}}{3-2} = \sqrt{3}-\sqrt{2}$

$\dfrac{1}{\sqrt{4}+\sqrt{3}} \times \dfrac{\sqrt{4}-\sqrt{3}}{\sqrt{4}-\sqrt{3}} = \dfrac{\sqrt{4}-\sqrt{3}}{4-3} = \sqrt{4}-\sqrt{3}$

....

$\dfrac{1}{\sqrt{9}+\sqrt{8}} \times \dfrac{\sqrt{9}-\sqrt{8}}{\sqrt{9}-\sqrt{8}} = \dfrac{\sqrt{9}-\sqrt{8}}{9-8} = \sqrt{9}-\sqrt{8}$

$\sqrt{2}-1+\sqrt{3}-\sqrt{2}+\sqrt{4}-\sqrt{3}+....+\sqrt{9}-\sqrt{8}$

$= -1 + 3 = 2.$

2. $246016 = 7936 \times 31 + 0.$

3. $x^0 = 1.$

4. $SI = \dfrac{x \times 6 \times 7}{2 \times 100} = \dfrac{21x}{100}$

$SI = \dfrac{(1200-x) \times 4 \times 7}{2 \times 100} = \dfrac{14(1200-x)}{100}$

According to the question,

$\dfrac{21x}{100} + \dfrac{14(1200-x)}{100} = 224$

$21x + 16800 - 14x = 224 \times 100$

$\Rightarrow \qquad 7x = 5600$

$\qquad\qquad x = 800$

$\therefore$ Amount lent at 6% = Rs 800.

5. $\qquad\qquad \dfrac{A}{B} = \dfrac{3}{4}$

$\qquad\qquad 3B = 4A$

$\qquad\qquad B = \dfrac{4A}{3} \qquad\qquad ...(i)$

Again $\qquad \dfrac{B}{C} = \dfrac{6}{7}$

$\qquad\qquad 7B = 6C$

$\qquad\qquad B = \dfrac{6C}{7} \qquad\qquad ...(ii)$

from (i) and (ii)

$\qquad\qquad \dfrac{4A}{3} = \dfrac{6C}{7}$

$\qquad\qquad 28A = 18C$

$\qquad\qquad \dfrac{A}{C} = \dfrac{18}{28} = \dfrac{9}{14}$

$\therefore \qquad\qquad A : C = 9 : 14.$

6. $\dfrac{25}{125} \times 100 = 20\%.$

7. $\because$ List Price = ₹ 160

first discount = 10%

Discount $= 160 \times \dfrac{10}{100} = $ ₹ 16

S.P. of article after 10% dis = 160 – 16

$\qquad\qquad\qquad\qquad = $ ₹ 144.

Let second discount = $x\%$

Dis $= 144 \times \dfrac{x}{100} = \dfrac{144x}{100}$

According to the question,

$\qquad 144 - \dfrac{144x}{100} = 122.40$

$\qquad \dfrac{14400 - 144x}{100} = \dfrac{12240}{100}$

$\qquad\qquad 144x = 2160$

$\qquad\qquad x = \dfrac{2160}{144} = 15$

$\therefore$ Second discount = 15%.

8. Let CP = Rs x

$\therefore \quad$ SP = $x + 80$

Profit = $x + 80 - x = $ ₹ 80

According to the question,

$\qquad 80 = \dfrac{2}{5}$ of x

$\therefore \qquad x = \dfrac{80 \times 5}{2} = 200$

The cost price of the toy = ₹ 200.

9. Let distance $= x$ km

Time taken at speed 25 km/hr $= \dfrac{x}{25}$ hrs.

Time taken at speed 30 km/hr $= \dfrac{x}{30}$ hrs.

According to the question,

$$\frac{x}{25} - \frac{x}{30} = \frac{1}{2} \Rightarrow \frac{6x - 5x}{150} = \frac{1}{2} \Rightarrow x = 75$$

$\therefore$ The length of the Journey = 75 km.

10.
$$\left[\frac{\sin 27°}{\cos(90 - 27°)}\right]^2 + \left[\frac{\sin(90 - 27°)}{\cos 27°}\right]^2 - 2 \times \frac{1}{2}$$

$$= \left(\frac{\sin 27°}{\sin 27°}\right)^2 + \left(\frac{\cos 27°}{\cos 27°}\right)^2 - 1$$

$$= 1 + 1 - 1 = 1.$$

11.
$$\frac{3\sin\theta}{\cos\theta} + \frac{\cos\theta}{\sin\theta} = \frac{5}{\sin\theta}$$

$$\frac{3\sin^2\theta + \cos^2\theta}{\cos\theta \cdot \sin\theta} = \frac{5}{\sin\theta}$$

$$3(1 - \cos^2\theta) + \cos^2\theta = 5\cos\theta$$

$$2\cos^2\theta + 5\cos\theta - 3 = 0$$

$$2\cos^2\theta + 6\cos\theta - \cos\theta - 3 = 0$$

$$2\cos\theta\,(\cos\theta + 3) - 1(\cos\theta + 3) = 0$$

$$(2\cos\theta - 1)\,(\cos\theta + 3) = 0$$

Either $\cos\theta = \dfrac{1}{2}$ or $\cos\theta = -3$ not possible.

$$\cos\theta = \cos 60°$$

$$\Rightarrow \quad \theta = 60°.$$

12.

Let AB is building and CD is tower.

In $\triangle$ABC,

$$\tan 60° = \frac{60}{x}$$

$$\sqrt{3} = \frac{60}{x}$$

$$x = \frac{60}{\sqrt{3}} \times \frac{\sqrt{3}}{\sqrt{3}} = 20\sqrt{3} \qquad \text{...(i)}$$

In $\triangle$BED,

$$\tan 30° = \frac{60 - h}{x}$$

$$\frac{1}{\sqrt{3}} = \frac{60 - h}{x}$$

$$x = \sqrt{3}\,(60 - h) \qquad \text{...(ii)}$$

from (i) and (ii)

$$\sqrt{3}\,(60 - h) = 20\sqrt{3}$$

$$h = 60 - 20$$

$$h = 40$$

$\therefore$ Height of the tower = 40 m.

13. The number 56 is used 3 times.

$\therefore$ mode = 56.

14. Let width of the verandah $= x$ m.

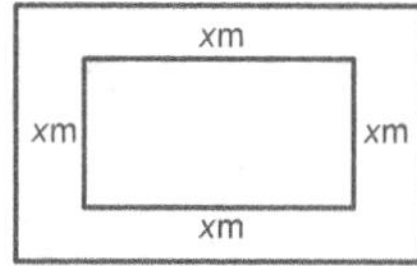

Area without verandah $= 5 \times 4 = 20$ m^2

Area with verandah $= (5 + x + x)\,(4 + x + x)$ m^2

According to the question,

$$(5 + 2x)\,(4 + 2x) = 20 + 22 = 42$$

$$20 + 10x + 8x + 4x^2 = 42$$

$$4x^2 + 18x - 22 = 0$$

$$2x^2 + 9x - 11 = 0$$

$$2x^2 + 11x - 2x - 11 = 0$$

$$x(2x + 11) - 1\,(2x + 11) = 0$$

$$(2x + 11)\,(x - 1) = 0$$

$$x = 1 \text{ or } x = \frac{-11}{2} \text{ not possible.}$$

$\therefore$ The width of the verandah = 1m.

15.

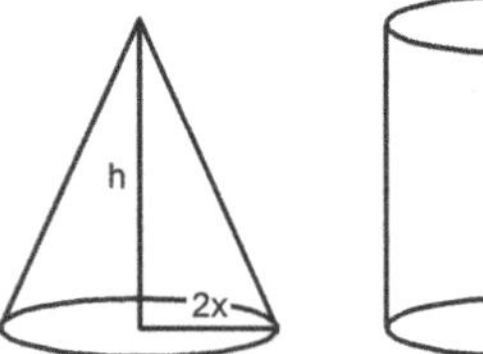

$$\frac{\text{Volume of cone}}{\text{Volume of cylinder}} = \frac{1}{3}\frac{\pi(2x)^2 \times h}{\pi x^2 \times h} = 4:3.$$

16. Volume of the cone = Volume of sphere

$$\frac{1}{3}\pi(2)^2 \times 8 = \frac{4}{3}\pi r^3$$

$$32 = 4r^3 \Rightarrow r = 2$$

$\therefore$ The diameter of the sphere = 4 cm.

17.

x	f	fx
10	3	30
15	10	150
20	x	$20x$
25	7	175
35	5	175
	$x+25$	$20x+530$

$$\text{Mean} = \frac{20x+530}{x+25}$$

$$20.6 = \frac{20x+530}{x+25}$$

$$20.6x + 515 = 20x + 530$$

$$x = \frac{15 \times 10}{6} = 25.$$

18. At least one head = {HH, HT, TH}

Number of favourable ways = 3

$\therefore$ Required probability = $\dfrac{3}{4}$.

19. All boys are not students
i.e., Some boys are students.
Some students are not employed
i.e., Some students are employed.

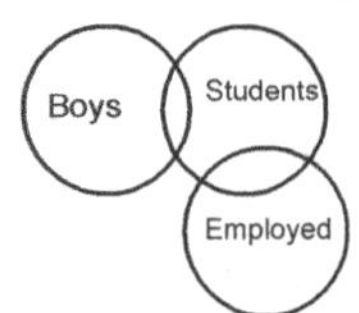

or,

20.

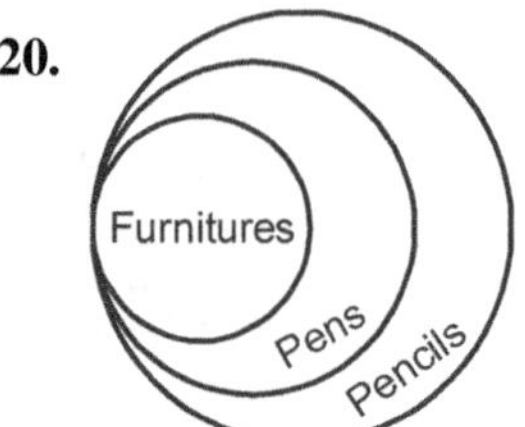

21.

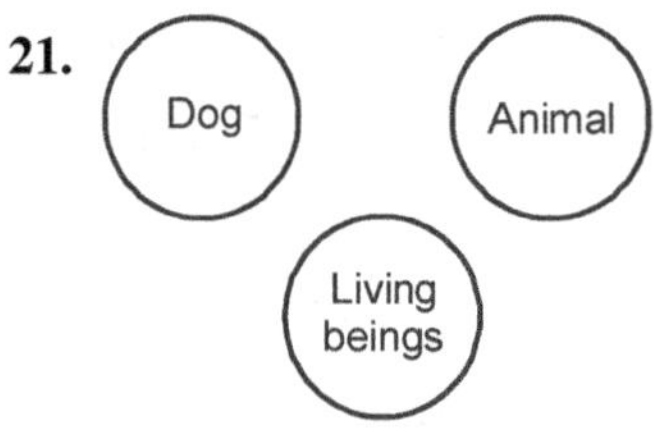

or,

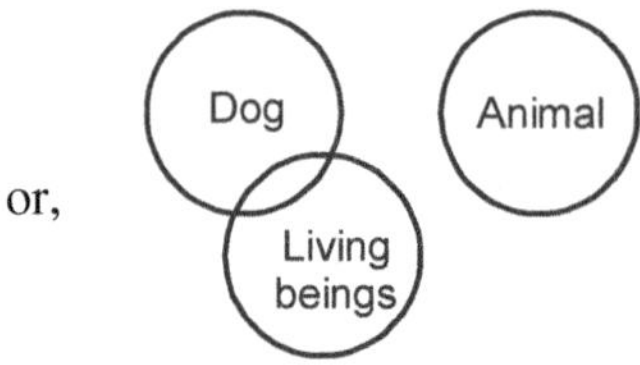

22. In the statement it has not said that only bird has not wings. Hence, we can not say that wingless beings are bird.

In the second statement it has said that all birds are rational, *i.e.,* some rationals are birds.

Hence, only conclusion (II) follows.

23. 5   7   10   15   15   20   [20]
   +5   +5   +5
     +8   +5

24.

$$\frac{2+1}{\sqrt{5}\times\sqrt{5}} = \frac{3}{5}$$

$$\frac{3+1}{5\times\sqrt{5}} = \frac{4}{5\sqrt{5}}, \quad \frac{4+1}{5\sqrt{5}\times\sqrt{5}} = \frac{5}{25},$$

$$\frac{5+1}{25\times\sqrt{5}} = \frac{6}{25\sqrt{5}}.$$

25. 3   15   39   75   [123]
  +12 +24 +36 +48

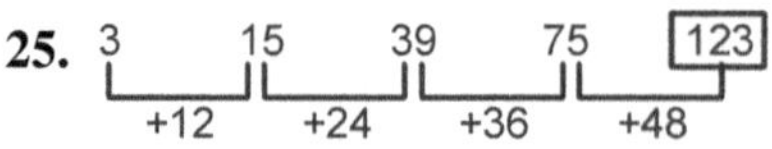

26. 25   25   27   22   30   19   34   16   [39]
  +2   +3   +4   +5
    −3   −3   −3

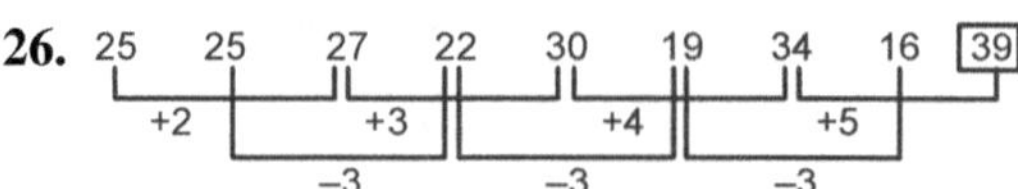

RRB—Railway Recruitment Board

Assistant Loco Pilot (ALP) & Technicians,

Recruitment Examination

FIRST STAGE COMPUTER BASED TEST (CBT)

1. Which of the following is not a prime number—
A. 1   B. 2
C. 131   D. 157

2. Express 36 as a product of prime number—
A. $2 \times 3 \times 6$ B. 6×6
C. $2 \times 2 \times 3 \times 3$ D. 4×9

3. Complete the series—
1, 2, 4, 7, 13, 24, 44, ?
A. 81   B. 80
C. 64   D. 66

4. The value of $(4^2)^3$ is—
A. $4 \times 2 \times 3$ B. 16×3
C. 4^3 D. 4^6

5. One of the factors of $6x^2 - 19x - 36$ is $(3x + 4)$. State the other factor—
A. $(2x - 9)$ B. $(6x - 19)$
C. $(6x - 9)$ D. $(2x - 19)$

6. If $3x^2 + 5x - 2 = 0$, find the value of x—
A. $\frac{1}{3}$ or -2 B. $\frac{1}{3}$ or 2
C. $-\frac{1}{3}$ or 2 D. $-\frac{1}{3}$ or -2

7. The mean of reciprocals of x and y is equal to—
A. $\dfrac{2(x+y)}{xy}$ B. $\dfrac{2x}{x+y}$
C. $\dfrac{x+y}{2xy}$ D. $\dfrac{x+y}{x-y}$

8. If $(2x)^x = 512$, then x is equal to—
A. 2   B. 3
C. 4   D. 5

9. Find the sum of all numbers upto 100—
A. 4950   B. 5100
C. 5000   D. 5050

10. Log $\frac{1}{2} = ?$
A. $-\dfrac{1}{3}$ B. $\dfrac{1}{2}$
C. $-\dfrac{1}{2}$ D. $\dfrac{1}{3}$

11. $\sqrt{41 - \sqrt{21 + \sqrt{19 - \sqrt{9}}}} = ?$
A. 3   B. 5
C. 6   D. 6.4

12. The value of $\dfrac{\sqrt{3} + \sqrt{2}}{\sqrt{3} - \sqrt{2}}$ is—
A. $5 + 2\sqrt{6}$ B. $5 - 2\sqrt{6}$
C. $3 + \sqrt[2]{5}$ D. $3 - \sqrt[2]{5}$

13. What is the 20% of 30% of 40%?
A. 2.4%   B. 3.0%
C. 24%   D. 30%

14. A book publisher sold 250 books and had a gain equal to selling price of 50 books. Find profit per cent of the publisher.
A. 25   B. 20
C. 50   D. 10

15. 20 boys finish a work in 30 days, then 40 boys can finish in—
A. 20 days　　　　B. 10 days
C. 25 days　　　　D. 15 days

16. Which is correct?
A. $\log_1 (Mn) = \log a\ M + \log a\ n$
B. $\log a\ (M + n) = \log a\ M + \log a\ n$
C. $\log a\ (M - n) = \log a\ M - \log a\ n$
D. $\log a \left(\dfrac{M}{n}\right) = \log a\ M + \log a\ n$

17. The ratio of 1 hour and 15 minutes to 5 hours is—
A. 2 : 5　　　　B. 4 : 15
C. 3 : 8　　　　D. 1 : 4

18. If $\sin\theta = \dfrac{5}{13}$, then $\cot\theta$ is equal to—
A. $\dfrac{12}{5}$　　　　B. $\dfrac{13}{12}$
C. $\dfrac{13}{5}$　　　　D. $\dfrac{12}{13}$

Direction (Q. 19-23): *Find the best suited missing number from the given alternatives.*

19. 1, 4, 8, 11, 15, __?__, 22
A. 19　　　　B. 18
C. 20　　　　D. 17

20. 1, 4, 9, 16, __?__
A. 23　　　　B. 24
C. 25　　　　D. 30

21. 1, 2, 6, 24, __?__
A. 120　　　　B. 144
C. 30　　　　D. 140

22. 1, 3, 9, __?__, 81
A. 12　　　　B. 15
C. 27　　　　D. 25

23. A, E, __?__, O, U
A. F　　　　B. I
C. G　　　　D. L

Direction (Q. 24-28): *Three words are given, first two words are related. Find the appropriate word from the given options for third word.*

24. Taka : Bangladesh : : Rupiah : ?
A. Spain
B. Denmark
C. Indonesia
D. Malaysia

25. Ghalib : Poetry : : Picasso : ?
A. Drama　　　　B. Literature
C. Sculpture　　　　D. Painting

26. Tarlatan : Muslin : : Poplin : ?
A. Jute　　　　B. Wool
C. Cotton　　　　D. Rayon

27. Ottawa : Canada : : Canberra : ?
A. Argentina　　　　B. Switzerland
C. Austria　　　　D. Australia

28. King : Throne : : Rider : ?
A. Seat　　　　B. Saddle
C. Horse　　　　D. Chair

29. If UMESH is coded as 'FNVHS', POT will be coded as—
A. JLG　　　　B. KMG
C. KLG　　　　D. LKG

30. If BEAT is coded as YVZG, MILD will be coded as—
A. NORW　　　　B. ONRW
C. WORN　　　　D. NROW

31. If NUMBER is coded as UNBMRE, GHOST will be coded as—
A. HOGTS　　　　B. HGOTS
C. HGDST　　　　D. HGSOT

32. If RADIO is coded as UDGLR; PHOTO will be coded as—
A. OIPWR　　　　B. OTOPT
C. SKRWR　　　　D. SKPWR

33. If WORLD is coded as ASVPH; GLOBE will be coded as—
A. OJSH　　　　B. KPSFI
C. KPSIF　　　　D. KPSHE

34. If it was Saturday on day before yesterday, which day will it be two days after day after tomorrow.
A. Monday　　　　B. Tuesday
C. Sunday　　　　D. Friday

35. Out of the following words, which word will cover at serial no. 2 in the dictionary.
A. Practice   B. Practical
C. Practicable   D. Practise

36. Seven men eat 28 fruits in 4 minutes. How much will one man take to eat one fruit?
A. 4 minutes   B. 3 minutes
C. 20 seconds   D. 1 minute

37. Lime water contains—
A. Calcium carbonate
B. Calcium hydroxide
C. Calcium bicarbonate
D. Sodium sulphate

38. Which of the following represents a chemical change?
A. Evaporation of alcohol
B. Sublimation of iodine
C. Heating of a platinum wire in bunsen flame
D. Heating of mercuric oxide powder

39. Pencillin is obtained from—
A. Algae fungi   B. Fungi
C. Synthetics   D. None of these

40. Isotopes differ in—
A. Number of electrons
B. Number of protons
C. Number of neutrons
D. Protons and neutrons

41. The drug most widely used to relieve pain is—
A. Paracetamol   B. Aspirin
C. Morphine   D. Nimusulide

42. A person climbing a hill bends forward in order to—
A. Avoid slipping   B. Increase speed
C. Reduce fatigue   D. Increase stability

43. The technique used to transmit audio signals in television broadcast is—
A. Amplitude modulation
B. Frequency modulation
C. Pulse code modulation
D. Time division multiplexing

44. Which of the following is the most elastic?
A. carbon   B. rubber
C. glass   D. paper

45. Energy is measured in the same unit as that of—
A. Work   B. Power
C. Momentum   D. Inertia

46. A device used in converting a.c. current into d.c. is called—
A. Transformer   B. Rectifier
C. Induction coil   D. Dynamo

47. Which of the following blood group is universal recipient?
A. A   B. B
C. AB   D. O

48. Which of the following is most important for digestion?
A. Proteins   B. Milk
C. Fat   D. Vitamins

49. The human skull consists of—
A. 22 bones   B. 14 bones
C. 8 bones   D. None of these

50. The first life of earth came—
A. In water   B. On land
C. In air   D. On mountains

51. DNA is concentrated in the—
A. Microsome   B. Nucleus
C. Protoplasm   D. Chromatin

52. Why is 28th February is observed as National Science Day?
A. Birth of Dr. Bhabha
B. First Indian atomic explosion
C. The world came to know about Raman Effect
D. A SLVD-1 launched

53. Which of the following is neither an element nor a compound?
A. Air   B. Water
C. Glucose   D. Gold

54. Which of the following gas does not pollute air?
A. Carbon dioxide   B. Carbon monoxide
C. Nitrogen oxide   D. Sulphur dioxide

55. The planet nearest to sun is—
A. Mars   B. Mercury
C. Venus   D. Neptune

56. Thimpu is the capital of—
A. Sikkim
B. Meghalaya
C. Bhutan
D. Mizoram

57. Railways was introduced in India in the year—
A. 1901
B. 1883
C. 1853
D. 1908

58. Kolar gold mines are in the state of—
A. Madhya Pradesh
B. Karnataka
C. Tamil Nadu
D. Odisha

59. The novel 'Devdas' is written by—
A. Sharatchandra Chatterjee
B. Rabindranath Tagore
C. Prem Chandra
D. Bankimchandra Chattopadhyaya

60. Ballarpur is known for—
A. Writing paper
B. Coal mines
C. Fertilizers
D. Cement plant

61. India is a 'republic' because—
A. Democratic rule exists here
B. Its head of state (country) is elected
C. Its constitution is written
D. All of the above

62. The duration of 'Zero hour' in Lok Sabha is—
A. 15 minutes
B. Half-an-hour
C. One hour
D. Not-specified

63. Lakshadweep is a group of .... islands.
A. 22
B. 27
C. 32
D. 35

64. The Sikh Guru who faught against the Mughals was—
A. Guru Nanak Dev
B. Guru Arjun Dev
C. Guru Tegh Bahadur
D. Guru Gobind Singh

65. How many spokes are there in our national emblem 'Ashok Chakra'?
A. 12
B. 15
C. 20
D. 24

66. The first Indian film in colour was—
A. Jhansi ki Rani
B. Aan
C. Sairandhri
D. Ramrajya

67. British shifted their capital from Calcutta to Delhi in—
A. 1905
B. 1909
C. 1911
D. 1914

68. Who gave the slogan 'Jai Hind'?
A. Mahatma Gandhi
B. Pandit Jawaharlal Nehru
C. Subhash Chandra Bose
D. Bhagat Singh

69. The number of seats allotted to different states in the Lok Sabha is determined on the basis of state's—
A. Population
B. Size
C. Resources
D. Location

70. The Andes Mountain range is in—
A. Europe
B. North America
C. Africa
D. South America

71. Konkan Railway runs between—
A. Mumbai-Manglore
B. Mumbai-Goa
C. Manglore-Trivandrum
D. Goa-Kanyakumari

72. The Indus Valley people had trade relations with—
A. Greece
B. Egypt
C. Ceylon
D. Mesopotamia

73. Which of the following is the highest mountain peak in South India:
A. Anai Mudi
B. Doda Beta
C. Mahendragiri
D. Dhupgarh

74. Which soil is more suitable for crops like cashew nut?
A. Red laterite soil
B. Black soil
C. Alluvial soil
D. Arid soil

75. If the duty on an article is reduced by 40% of its present rate, by how much percent must the consumption increase in order that the revenue remains unaltered?
A. $60\frac{2}{3}\%$
B. $64\frac{2}{3}\%$
C. $66\frac{2}{3}\%$
D. None of these

ANSWERS

1	2	3	4	5	6	7	8	9	10
A	C	A	D	A	A	C	B	D	B

11	12	13	14	15	16	17	18	19	20
C	A	A	B	D	A	D	A	B	C

21	22	23	24	25	26	27	28	29	30
A	C	B	C	D	C	D	B	C	D

31	32	33	34	35	36	37	38	39	40
D	C	B	D	B	D	A	C	B	C

41	42	43	44	45	46	47	48	49	50
B	D	B	A	A	D	B	D	B	A

51	52	53	54	55	56	57	58	59	60
B	C	A	C	B	C	C	B	A	A

61	62	63	64	65	66	67	68	69	70
D	C	D	C	D	C	C	C	A	D

71	72	73	74	75
C	D	A	A	C

EXPLANATORY ANSWERS

1. 1 is neither prime nor composit.

2. 2 and 3 are prime numbers.

4. $(4^2)^3$

$= (4)^{2 \times 3} = 4^6$

5. Dividing $6x^2 - 19x - 36$ by $(3x + 4)$

$$3x + 4 \overline{)6x^2 - 19x - 36} \, (2x - 9$$
$$\underline{6x^2 + 8x}$$
$$-27x - 36$$
$$\underline{-27x - 36}$$
$$\times \quad \times$$

So, other factor will be $2x - 9$.

6.
$$3x^2 + 5x - 2 = 0$$
$$\Rightarrow \quad 3x^2 + 6x - x - 2 = 0$$
$$\Rightarrow \quad 3x(x + 2) - 1(x + 2) = 0$$
$$\Rightarrow \quad (3x - 1)(x + 2) = 0$$
$$\Rightarrow \quad x = \frac{1}{3}, -2$$

7. Reciprocal of x and $y = \dfrac{1}{x}$ and $\dfrac{1}{y}$

$\therefore$ Mean of the reciprocal $= \dfrac{\frac{1}{x} + \frac{1}{y}}{2} = \dfrac{x + y}{2xy}$

8. Since $(2^x)^x = 512$

$\Rightarrow \quad (2^x)^x = 2^9 = (2^3)^3 \quad \Rightarrow \quad x = 3$

9. Sum of all numbers upto $100 = \dfrac{n(n+1)}{2}$

$= \dfrac{100 \times 101}{2} = 5050$

11. $\sqrt{41 - \sqrt{21 + \sqrt{19 - \sqrt{9}}}}$

$= \sqrt{41 - \sqrt{21 + \sqrt{19 - 3}}}$

$= \sqrt{41 - \sqrt{21 + \sqrt{16}}}$

$= \sqrt{41 - \sqrt{25}} = \sqrt{41 - 5} = \sqrt{36} = 6$

12.
$$\frac{\sqrt{3}+\sqrt{2}}{\sqrt{3}-\sqrt{2}} = \frac{\sqrt{3}+\sqrt{2}}{\sqrt{3}-\sqrt{2}} \times \frac{\sqrt{3}+\sqrt{2}}{\sqrt{3}+\sqrt{2}}$$

$$= \frac{\left(\sqrt{3}\right)^2 + \left(\sqrt{2}\right)^2 + 2\sqrt{6}}{3-2}$$

$$= 5 + 2\sqrt{6}$$

14. On selling 250 books their is a gain of 50 books

$\therefore$ On selling 1 book their is a gain of $\dfrac{50}{250}$

$\therefore$ On selling 100 books their is a gain of

$$\frac{50}{250} \times 100 = 20\%$$

18. Given $\sin\theta = \dfrac{5}{13}$

$$\cos\theta = \sqrt{1-\left(\frac{5}{13}\right)^2} = \sqrt{1-\frac{25}{169}}$$

$$= \sqrt{\frac{144}{169}}$$

$\therefore \quad \cot\theta = \dfrac{\cos\theta}{\sin\theta} = \dfrac{\frac{12}{13}}{\frac{5}{13}} = \dfrac{12}{5}$.

19.

$1+3 = 4,$	$4+4 = 8$
$8+3 = 11,$	$11+4 = 15$
$15+3 = \boxed{18},$	$28+4 = 22$

20.

$1^2 = 1,$	$2^2 = 4,$
$3^2 = 9,$	$4^2 = 16$
$5^2 = \boxed{25}$	

21.

$1 \times 2 = 2,$	$2 \times 3 = 6,$
$6 \times 4 = 24$	$24 \times 5 = \boxed{120}$

29. 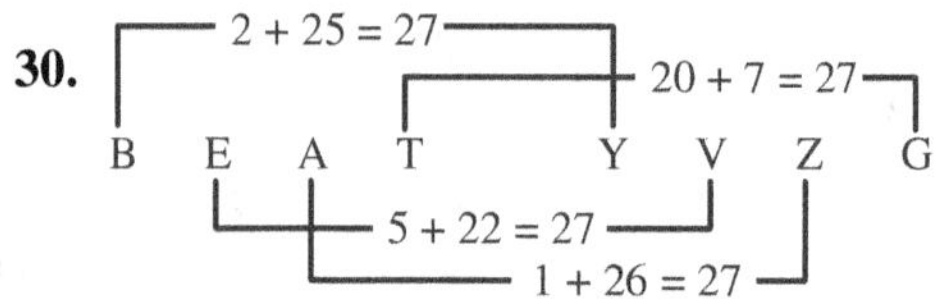

Hence, POT will be coded as KLG.

30.

Hence, MILD will be coded as NROW.

31.
N   U   M   B   E   R

U   N   B   M   R   E

Hence, GHOST will be coded as HGSOT.

34.

Saturday Sunday Monday Tuesday Wednesday Thursday $\boxed{\text{Friday}}$

Day before Yesterday — Yesterday — Today — Tomorrow — Day after tomorrow — One day after day after tomorrow — Tow day after day after tomorrow

36. Required time $= \dfrac{4 \times 7}{28} = 1$ minute.

RRB—Railway Recruitment Board

Assistant Loco Pilot (ALP) & Technicians,

Recruitment Examination

FIRST STAGE COMPUTER BASED TEST (CBT)

1. Find the value of

$$\frac{a^2 - b^2}{a - b} - \frac{a^3 - b^3}{a^2 - b^2}$$

  A. $\dfrac{a+b}{ab}$ B. $\dfrac{a-b}{ab}$

  C. $\dfrac{ab}{a+b}$ D. $\dfrac{ab}{a-b}$

2. Some people collected 72 rupees by giving equal amount. If three persons were less then each had to give 4 rupees more. How many people were there?

  A. 8   B. 9

  C. 12   D. 24

3. If $25^{n-1} = 5^{2n-1} - 100$, then what is the value of n?

  A. 0   B. 1

  C. 2   D. –1

4. The difference of simple interest and recurring interest of any amount in 3 years by the rate of 10% is ₹ 31. What will be the principal amount?

  A. 1331   B. 1200

  C. 1000   D. 800

5. There are 5 : 2 ratio of milk and water in any mixture of 35 litre. If 5 litre more milk is mixed in it then what will be the ratio of milk and water in the new?

  A. 3 : 1   B. 25 : 10

  C. 30 : 25   D. 2 : 7

6. If the speed of a passenger train is enhanced with 10 km per hour, then it takes 3 hours less time to cover a distance of 360 km. Find the average speed of the train.

  A. 25 km/hour   B. 30 km/hour

  C. 40 km/hour   D. 60 km/hour

7. If 25 people finished one project in 15 days doing 8 hours job, then how many days will be taken by 20 people for doing two-times more job?

  A. 50 days   B. 40 days

  C. 30 days   D. 25 days

8. Monthly average income of a person (January, February and March) was 1500 rupees, and monthly average income of February, March and April was 1800 rupees. If his income of April is 1600 then what was his January's income?

  A. ₹ 700   B. ₹ 800

  C. ₹ 1000   D. ₹ 1200

9. A person buys two pen in 150 rupees, he sells one of them at 12% profit and the other at 12% loss. He realises that he has sold both of them at same price, then what will be the ratio of buying price of both pen?

  A. 1 : 2   B. 3 : 2

  C. 4 : 5   D. 11 : 14

10. If $\sec\theta = \dfrac{5}{4}$, then what will be the value of

$$\frac{\sec\theta - 2\cos\theta}{\tan\theta - \cot\theta} \, .$$

  A. $\dfrac{7}{12}$ B. $\dfrac{3}{5}$

  C. $\dfrac{1}{12}$ D. $\dfrac{1}{7}$

11. What will be the value of tan 5° tan 10° tan 45° tan 80° tan 85°?

  A. 0   B. 1

  C. –1   D. 2

12. Angle of elevation of top of a high building and a helicopter flying right above the building are 30° and 60° respectively from a point 'P' on the ground. Find out the height of helicopter from ground.

  A. 30 metre   B. 45 metre

  C. 60 metre   D. 70 metre

13. Mean of 11 numbers is 35. If the mean of first 6 number and the mean of last 6 numbers are gradually 32 and 37, then what will be the 6th number?

  A. 27   B. 28

  C. 29   D. 30

14. If the length of any rectangle is increased by 50% and the breadth decreased by 50%, a new rectangle is formed, what will be the area of a new rectangle?

  A. 50% less than first rectangle

  B. 50% more than first rectangle

  C. 25% more than first rectangle

  D. 25% less than first rectangle

15. If the radius of any circle is increased by two times then what will increase in its surface area?

  A. 400%   B. 300%

  C. 200%   D. 100%

16. Ratio of radius and height of a right circular cone is 5 : 12. If volume of the cone is 314 cm³ then find the slant height of the cone?

  A. 13 cm   B. 12 cm

  C. 8 cm   D. 5 cm

17. Sixth and seventh observations of twelve observations which are arranged in an increasing order are 14 and 15, then what is the median of all the twelve observations?

  A. 14.5

  B. 14

  C. 15

  D. 15.5

18. What is the distance of a pt. (1, 2) from the mid pt. of a line segment joining (6, 8) and (2, 4)?

  A. 4   B. 5

  C. 6   D. 8

Direction (Q. 19-22): *Select the right answer in the following series?*

19. 5, 10, 30, ..., 600

  A. 50   B. 60

  C. 120   D. 200

20. 42, 24, 53, 35, 64, ...

  A. 46   B. 48

  C. 75   D. None of these

21. 0, 7, 26, 63, ...

  A. 93   B. 103

  C. 121   D. 124

22. B, ..., J, P, V

  A. C   B. F

  C. G   D. H

Direction (Q. 23-26): *There is a code for each english word. Choose the right option on the basis of code, from the given options.*

23. Code 'CZMBD' is for 'DANCE', then what will be for 'ENGLISH'?

  A. FMHMJTI

  B. DMFKHRG

  C. CLFKHRG

  D. DOHKHRG

24. Code 'WVZI' is for 'DEAR' then what will be for 'PALE'?

  A. KZOV   B. KAOU

  C. VZOV   D. KZOU

25. Code 'UVTKMG' is for 'STRIKE' then the code 'KMLMBW' will be for which word?

  A. MONDAY

  B. IONOZU

  C. MONODY

  D. IKJKZU

26. Code 'IDHEL' is for 'DELHI' then what will be for 'TUFAN'?

  A. TNAUF   B. NATUF

  C. NTAUF   D. NTUAF

27. If 14 February comes 4 days prior to Monday in a superannuation, then which day will be on 17 March?
A. Monday B. Tuesday
C. Wednesday D. Sunday

28. First E is as far as second E in the word 'PRECIPITATE', give the name of that letter which is situated at the same distance from the third letter in the English alphabet.
A. J B. K
C. L D. M

Direction (Q. 29-32): *Read the following passage.*

When Varun born, his father Tarun was 30. Paternal aunt of Varun, Urvashi is 3 year younger than her brother Tarun and 5 year younger than her husband Yogesh. There are three children of Yogesh and Urvashi–Kamal, Jalaj and Vaishali. Kamal born on his father's 28th birthday. After 10 year his brother Jalaj is of less than 7 years of half of his father and his sister Vaishali will be of 1/3 of her mother's age. Kamal was born 12 years earlier.

29. Which one is correct in descending order, according to age?
A. Yogesh, Kamal, Varun, Vaishali
B. Tarun, Yogesh, Vaishali, Varun
C. Urvashi, Yogesh, Varun, Vaishali
D. Jalaj, Vaishali, Kamal, Varun.

30. Which one is correct in ascending order according to age?
A. Varun, Vaishali, Jalaj, Kamal
B. Varun, Tarun, Urvashi, Vaishali
C. Vaishali, Jalaj, Kamal, Urvashi
D. Vaishali, Kamal, Jalaj, Varun

31. Elder sister of Varun, Sarita can be younger than—
A. Vaishali
B. Kamal and Vaishali
C. Jalaj
D. Urvashi

32. Who among the family is younger than as many people, as he is elder?
A. Vaishali B. Kamal
C. Varun D. Jalaj

Direction (Q. 33-35): *There are some problematic figures and after that four options are given. There is one figure which is in order of problematic figure. Choose the figure.*

33. 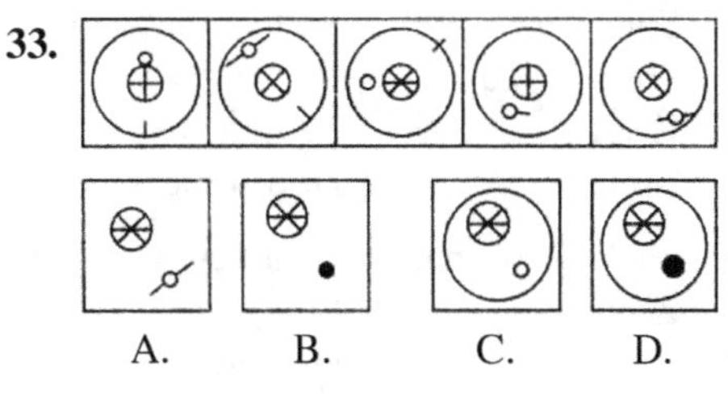
A. B. C. D.

34. 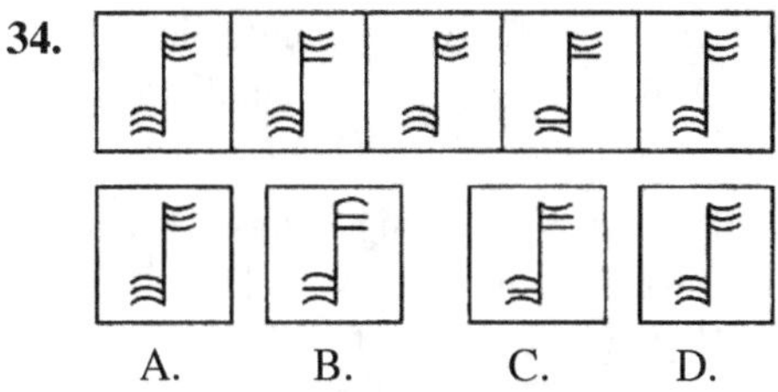
A. B. C. D.

35. 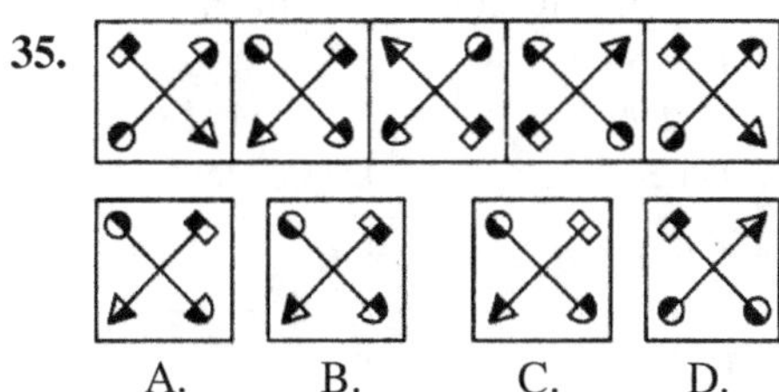
A. B. C. D.

Direction (Q. 36): *Two conclusion I and II are given in the following question which are derived from first two statement. Assume that both statement are true and decide whether the conclusions are correct or not. Choose the right option.*

36. Statement:
No one human is animal.
Some animals are intelligent.
Conclusion:
I. Some human are intelligent.
II. Some intelligent are human.
A. Only I is true
B. Only II is true
C. I and II both are true
D. No one is true

37. Jaundice is due to the infection of—
A. Brain B. Liver
C. Kidney D. Spleen

38. In a normal person average rate of heart beat is—
A. 82   B. 92
C. 72   D. 98

39. EEG is used for the observation of which part of the body?
A. Heart   B. Lungs
C. Brain   D. Muscles

40. Colour of cows milk is light yellow due to—
A. Zenthophil   B. Riboflavin
C. Ribulos   D. Kerotin

41. Which of the following is infectious—
A. Diabetes   B. Diphtheria
C. Arthritis   D. Cancer

42. Which of the following is less in Anaemia?
A. Haemoglobin   B. Collagen
C. Highoglobin   D. Myosin

43. Which of the following disease spreads through air?
A. Plague   B. Typhoid
C. Tuberculosis   D. Cholera

44. Cereals are rich sources of—
A. Starch   B. Glucose
C. Fructose   D. Maltose

45. Aspirin is the ordinary name of—
A. Salicylic Acid
B. Salicylate
C. Methyl Salicylate
D. Acetylsalicylic Acid

46. Reason of small Pox is—
A. Rubiola Virus   B. Variola Virus
C. Varicela   D. Mixovirus

47. Carbon Monoxide is an inflammable gas. Which of the following is also an inflammable gas—
A. Helium   B. Nitrogen
C. Oxygen   D. Hydrogen

48. In the Aerobic Respiration which of the following is needed—
A. Heat   B. Water
C. Oxygen   D. Sunlight

49. Which of the following does not produce Hydrogen in reaction with water?
A. Potassium   B. Cadmium
C. Sodium   D. Lithium

50. Ozone contains—
A. Only Oxygen
B. Oxygen and Nitrogen
C. Hydrogen and Carbon
D. Oxygen and Carbon

51. Which of the following liquid is of low density?
A. Fresh water   B. Salt water
C. Petrol   D. Mercury

52. Which of the following theory is used to produce low-temperature?
A. Super conductivity
B. Joule-Kelvin effect
C. Thermoelectric effect
D. Adiabatic demagnetisation

53. Photoelectric cell transforms—
A. Mechanical energy into electrical energy
B. Heat energy into mechanical energy
C. Light energy into chemical energy
D. Light energy into electrical energy

54. Two stones of different masses if fallen down from the peak of the building—
A. small stone reaches before on the ground
B. big stone reaches before on the ground
C. both stones reach together on the ground
D. it depends on the construction of stones

55. Three bigha corridor combines—
A. India and Pakistan
B. India and China
C. Bangladesh and Pakistan
D. Bangladesh and India

56. Who built the Vijay Stambh in Chittor?
A. Maharana Pratap
B. Rana Sangram Singh
C. Rana Kumbha
D. Rana Ratan Singh

57. Which religious book was called as 'mother' by Gandhiji?
A. Ramayana

B. The New Testament
C. Bhagvatgeeta
D. Kuran Sharif

58. Tihari water electrical complex is situated on the bank of river—
A. Alaknanda   B. Mandakini
C. Dhauli Ganga   D. Bhagirathi

59. The person who had made the design of Rashtrapati Bhawan was—
A. Adward Stone   B. Le Kaburje
C. Advin Lutians   D. Tarun Dutta

60. 'Quit India' movement 1942 was commenced in the month of—
A. January   B. March
C. August   D. December

61. Match the following—
Group-I
(a) Keshav Chandra Sen
(b) Dayanand Saraswati
(c) Atmaram Pandurang
(d) Syed Ahmed Khan
Group-II
1. Prarthana Samaj
2. Brahma Samaj
3. Aligarh Movement
4. Arya Samaj

	(a)	(b)	(c)	(d)
A.	4	1	3	2
B.	1	4	2	3
C.	2	4	1	3
D.	3	2	4	1

62. Who was the first British President of Indian National Congress?
A. George Yule   B. William Vederbern
C. A.O. Hume   D. Henery Coton

63. Which person is known as 'Grand old man of India'?
A. Bal Gangadhar Tilak
B. Dada Bhai Nauroji
C. Moti Lal Nehru
D. Lala Lajpat Rai

64. Who wrote the 'Akbarnama'?
A. Akbar   B. Birbal
C. Abul Fajal   D. Bhagwan Das

65. In India, Panchayati Raj System was introduced—
A. In 1950   B. In 1945
C. In 1959   D. In 1962

66. The person who was elected twice as the Vice-President was—
A. Dr. S. Radhakrishnan
B. Shri R. Venkat Raman
C. Dr. Shankar Dayal Sharma
D. Shri V. V. Giri

67. By which amendment of Indian constitution two words - Socialist and Secular was added in the Preamble?
A. 28   B. 40
C. 42   D. 52

68. Indian constitution adhered to—
A. 26 January, 1950
B. 26 January, 1952
C. 15 August, 1948
D. 26 November, 1949

69. Who was the first lady governor of a state in free India?
A. Smt. Sarojini Naidu
B. Smt. Sucheta Kriplani
C. Smt. Indira Gandhi
D. Smt. Vijaya Luxmi Pandit

70. Name the parliamentary committee which scrutinizes the report of Comptroller and Auditor General.
A. Estimates Committee
B. Select Committee
C. Public Accounts Committee
D. None of these

71. Which of the following shows the joining line of the places where rainfall are equal?
A. Iisohips   B. Iisohelienj
C. Isobar   D. Isohytes

72. Equator line is—
A. the line which joins the North and South pole
B. the imaginary line which moves exactly in the centre of the earth of North and South Pole
C. A girdle around Saturn (planet)
D. An axis of rotation of earth

73. An article cost ₹ 80 to the vendor. If he marks the article for 50% more than the cost price and sells it 25% less than the marked price. What is his gain percentage?

A. 25%

B. $21\dfrac{1}{4}\%$

C. $12\dfrac{1}{2}\%$

D. $15\dfrac{1}{2}\%$

74. $100 \times 10 - 100 + 2000 \div 100 = ?$

A. 840   B. 920

C. 760   D. None of these

75. Pipe 'A' can fill a tank in 10 hours and pipe 'B' can fill the same tank in 12 hours. Both the pipes are opened to fill the tank and after 3 hours pipe 'A' is closed. Pipe 'B' will fill the remaining part of the tank in:

A. 5 hours 36 minutes

B. 5 hours 24 minutes

C. 5 hours 39 minutes

D. 5 hours 48 minutes

ANSWERS

1	2	3	4	5	6	7	8	9	10
C	B	C	C	A	B	C	A	D	B
11	**12**	**13**	**14**	**15**	**16**	**17**	**18**	**19**	**20**
B	A	C	D	B	A	A	B	C	A
21	**22**	**23**	**24**	**25**	**26**	**27**	**28**	**29**	**30**
D	D	B	A	C	C	B	B	A	C
31	**32**	**33**	**34**	**35**	**36**	**37**	**38**	**39**	**40**
B	B	C	C	A	D	B	C	C	D
41	**42**	**43**	**44**	**45**	**46**	**47**	**48**	**49**	**50**
B	A	A	A	D	B	D	C	B	A
51	**52**	**53**	**54**	**55**	**56**	**57**	**58**	**59**	**60**
C	A	D	C	D	C	C	D	C	C
61	**62**	**63**	**64**	**65**	**66**	**67**	**68**	**69**	**70**
C	A	B	C	C	A	C	A	A	C
71	**72**	**73**	**74**	**75**					
D	B	C	B	B					

EXPLANATORY ANSWERS

1.
$$\frac{a^2-b^2}{a-b} - \frac{a^3-b^3}{a^2-b^2}$$
$$= \frac{(a+b)(a-b)}{a-b} - \frac{\left[(a-b)(a^2+ab+b^2)\right]}{(a+b)(a-b)}$$
$$= a+b - \frac{(a^2+ab+b^2)}{a+b}$$
$$= \frac{a^2+2ab+b^2-a^2-ab-b^2}{a+b} = \frac{ab}{a+b}.$$

2. Let no. people $= x$

According to the question
$$x \times y = 72 \quad \ldots(i)$$
$$\Rightarrow \quad y = \frac{72}{x}$$

Now, $(x-3)(y+4) = 72$
$$\Rightarrow xy + 4x - 3y - 12 = 72 \quad \ldots(ii)$$

From (i) and (ii)
$$xy = xy + 4x - 3y - 12$$

$\Rightarrow \qquad 4x - 3y = 12$

$$4x - 3\left(\frac{72}{x}\right) = 12$$

$\Rightarrow \qquad 4x^2 - 216 = 12x$

$\Rightarrow \quad 4x^2 - 12x - 216 = 0$

$\Rightarrow \qquad x^2 - 3x - 54 = 0$

$\Rightarrow \quad x^2 - 9x + 6x - 54 = 0$

$\Rightarrow x(x - 9) + 6(x - 9) = 0$

$\Rightarrow \qquad (x - 9)(x + 6) = 0$

either $x = 9$ or $x = -6$ (not possible)

$\therefore$ Required no. of people = 9.

3. $25^{n-1} = 5^{2n-1} - 100$

$\Rightarrow \qquad 5^{2n-1} - 25^{n-1} = 100$

$\Rightarrow \quad \dfrac{5^{2n}}{5} - (5^2)^{(n-1)} = 100$

$\Rightarrow \qquad \dfrac{5^{2n}}{5} - 5^{2n-1} = 100$

$\Rightarrow \qquad \dfrac{5^{2n}}{5} - \dfrac{5^{2n}}{25} = 100$

$\Rightarrow \qquad \dfrac{5 \times 5^{2n} - 5^{2n}}{25} = 100$

$\Rightarrow \qquad 5^{2n}[5 - 1] = 2500$

$\Rightarrow \qquad 5^{2n} = \dfrac{2500}{4} = 625$

$\Rightarrow \qquad 5^{2n} = (5)^4$

$\Rightarrow \qquad 2n = 4$

$\Rightarrow \qquad n = 2$

4. Let principal = ₹ 100

$$SI = \frac{100 \times 10 \times 3}{100} = ₹\ 30$$

$$A = P\left(1 + \frac{r}{100}\right)^t$$

$$= 100\left(1 + \frac{10}{100}\right)^3 = 100 \times \left(\frac{11}{10}\right)^3$$

$$= \frac{1331}{10}$$

$$C.I. = A - P = \frac{1331}{10} - 100$$

$$= \frac{331}{10} = 33.1$$

C.I. – S.I. = 33.1 – 30 = 3.1

when diff. is ₹ 3.1 then P = ₹ 100

when diff. is ₹ 31 then P = $\dfrac{100}{3.1} \times 31$

$$= \frac{100}{31} \times 31 \times 10$$

$\therefore \qquad$ P = ₹ 1000.

5. Amount of milk = $\dfrac{5}{7} \times 35 = 25$ litre

Amount of water = $\dfrac{2}{7} \times 35 = 10$ litre

Now,

Amount of milk = 25 + 5 = 30 litre

Amount of water = 10 litre

$\therefore$ Ratio of milk and water in the new mixture

$$= 30 : 10$$

$$= 3 : 1.$$

6. Let the average speed of the train = x km/hr

According to the question,

$$\frac{360}{x} - \frac{360}{x+10} = 3$$

$\Rightarrow \qquad \dfrac{360(x+10-x)}{x(x+10)} = 3$

$\Rightarrow \ x^2 + 10x - 1200 = 0$

$\Rightarrow \ (x + 40)(x - 30) = 0$

$\Rightarrow x = -40$ or $x = 30$

$\therefore$ Required speed = 30 km/hr.

8. Jan. + Feb. + March = 1500 × 3 = 4500

Feb. + March + April = 1800 × 3 = 5400

Feb. + March = 5400 – 1600 = 3800

$\therefore$ January's income = 4500 – 3800 = ₹ 700.

10. $\because \sec\theta = \dfrac{5}{4} = \dfrac{h}{b} \quad \therefore p = 3$

$$\cos\theta = \frac{b}{h} = \frac{4}{5}$$

$$\tan\theta = \frac{p}{b} = \frac{3}{4}, \quad \cot\theta = \frac{b}{p} = \frac{4}{3}$$

Now,

$$\frac{\sec\theta - 2\cos\theta}{\tan\theta - \cot\theta} = \frac{\dfrac{5}{4} - 2\times\dfrac{4}{5}}{\dfrac{3}{4} - \dfrac{4}{3}}$$

$$= \frac{\dfrac{5}{4} - \dfrac{8}{5}}{\dfrac{9-16}{12}} = \frac{\dfrac{25-32}{20}}{-\dfrac{7}{12}} = -\frac{7}{20} \times -\frac{12}{7} = \frac{12}{20} = \frac{3}{5}.$$

11. $\tan 5° \cdot \tan 10° \cdot \tan 45° \cdot \tan 80° \cdot \tan 85°$

$= \tan 5° \times \tan(90-5)° \times \tan 10° \cdot \tan(90-10)° \times \tan 45°$

$= \tan 5° \times \cot 5° \times \tan 10° \times \cot 10° \times \tan 45°$

$= 1 \times 1 \times 1 = 1.$

13. Required 6th number $= (32 \times 6 + 37 \times 6) - (35 \times 11)$

$= 6(32 + 37) - 385$

$= 6 \times 69 - 385$

$= 414 - 385 = 29.$

14. Tricky Method

Percentage increase in the length of rectangle $= 50\%$

and percentage decrease in the breadth of rectangle $= 50\%$

$\therefore$ Percentage increase or decrease in the area of the rectangle $= \left[50 - 50 + \dfrac{50\times(-50)}{100}\right]\%$

$= -\dfrac{2500}{100}\% = -25\%$

Since negative (–) sign indicate decrease.
Hence, the area will decrease by 25%.

15. Area of circle $= \pi r^2$

Now, area of circle $= \pi(2r)^2 = 4\pi r^2$

Area increased $= 4\pi r^2 - \pi r^2 = 3\pi r^2$

Percentage increased area

$$= \frac{3\pi r^2}{\pi r^2} \times 100 = 300\%.$$

16. Let radius of cone $= 5x$ cm

and height of cone $= 12\,x$ cm

volume of cone $= \dfrac{1}{3}\pi(5x)^2 \times 12x$

$\Rightarrow \dfrac{1}{3} \times \dfrac{22}{7} \times 25x^2 \times 12x = 314$

$\Rightarrow \quad 3.14 \times 100\,x^3 = 314$

$\Rightarrow \qquad\qquad 314\,x^3 = 314$

$\Rightarrow \qquad\qquad\quad x^3 = 1$

$\Rightarrow \qquad\qquad\quad x = 1$

$\therefore \qquad$ Radius $= 5x = 5 \times 1 = 5$ cm

height $= 12x$

$= 12 \times 1 = 12$ cm

slant height $= \sqrt{(5)^2 + (12)^2} = \sqrt{169}$

$= 13$ cm.

17. Here $n = 12$ which is even number

$$\therefore \text{ median} = \left[\frac{\dfrac{n}{2}\text{th term} + \text{next term}}{2}\right]$$

$$= \left[\frac{6\text{th term} + 7\text{th term}}{2}\right]$$

$$= \frac{14+15}{2} = \frac{29}{2} = 14.5.$$

RRB—Railway Recruitment Board
Assistant Loco Pilot (ALP) & Technicians,
Recruitment Examination

FIRST STAGE COMPUTER BASED TEST (CBT)

1. The value of

$$\frac{a\sqrt{a}+b\sqrt{b}}{\left(\sqrt{a}+\sqrt{b}\right)(a-b)} + \frac{2\sqrt{b}}{\sqrt{a}+\sqrt{b}} - \frac{\sqrt{ab}}{a-b} \text{ is—}$$

A. 0   B. 1

C. $\sqrt{ab}$ D. $\left(\sqrt{a}+\sqrt{b}\right)$

2. In a mixture of 35 litres, the ratio of milk and water is 5 : 2. Another 5 litres of milk is added to the mixture. The ratio of milk and water in the new mixture is—

A. 3 : 1   B. 1 : 3
C. 2 : 3   D. 3 : 2

3. Walking at 4 km an hour, a peon reaches his office 5 minutes late. If he walks at 5 km an hour, he will be 4 minutes too early. The distance of his office from the residence is—

A. 5 km   B. 4 km
C. 3 km   D. 2 km

4. If $5^{x-2} \cdot 3^{2x-3} = 135$, then the value of x is—

A. 0   B. 1
C. 2   D. 3

5. The simple interest on a certain amount at 4% p.a. for 4 years is ₹ 80 more than the interest on the same sum for 3 years at 5% p.a. The sum is—

A. ₹ 6000   B. ₹ 7200
C. ₹ 7500   D. ₹ 8000

6. A trader marks an article at 30% more than the cost price. He gives 10% discount to his customers and gains ₹ 25.50 per article. The cost price of the article is—

A. ₹ 150   B. ₹ 200
C. ₹ 175   D. ₹ 250

7. The price of sugar is increased by 25%. How much per cent should a man decrease his consumption so that there is no increase in his expenditure?

A. 10%   B. 20%
C. 5%   D. 15%

8. ₹ 6500 were divided equally among a certain number of persons. Had there been 15 more persons each would have got ₹ 30 less. The original number of persons was—

A. 65   B. 60
C. 50   D. 40

9. 2 men and 6 boys can do in 4 days a piece of work which would be done again in 4 days by 4 men and 3 boys. One man will do it in—

A. 36 days   B. 24 days
C. 16 days   D. 12 days

10. If sin A = 24/25, the value of tan A + sec A, where $0° < A < 90°$ is—

A. 49   B. 25
C. 24   D. 7

11. If tan A = n sin B and sin A = m sin B, then the value of $\cos^2$ A is—

A. m^2/n^2 B. $m^2 \times n^2$
C. $m^2 - n^2$ D. $m^2 + n^2$

12. The angle of elevation of the top of a hill at the foot of a tower is 60° and the angle of elevation of the top of the tower from the foot of the hill is 30°. If the tower is 50 m high, the height of the hill is—

A. 100 m   B. 125 m
C. 150 m   D. 200 m

(1958) Practice Papers—7

13. A steel wire when bent in the form of a square encloses an area of 121 sq. cm. If the same wire is bent into the form of a circle, the area of the circle is—
    A. 88 sq. cm
    B. 142 sq. cm
    C. 154 sq. cm
    D. 212 sq. cm

14. The number of spherical bullets that can be made out of a solid cube of lead whose edge measures 44 cm, if the diameter of each bullet be 4 cm, is—
    A. 2541
    B. 847
    C. 1270
    D. 363

15. The ratio between the radius of the base and the height of a cylinder is 2 : 3. If its volume is 1617 cm^3, the total surface area of the cylinder is—
    A. 575 cm^2
    B. 770 cm^2
    C. 1205 cm^2
    D. 1500 cm^2

16. The median of the following data is—
    25, 34, 31, 23, 22, 26, 35, 26, 20, 32
    A. 25.5
    B. 26
    C. 26.5
    D. 25

17. The average weight of 10 men is decreased by 3 kg when one of them whose weight is 80 kg is replaced by a new person. The weight of the new person is—
    A. 70 kg
    B. 60 kg
    C. 50 kg
    D. 73 kg

18. The value of k so that the points A (k, 1), B (2, 1) and C (5, –1) are collinear is—
    A. 4
    B. 3
    C. 2
    D. 1

Directions (Qs. 19 to 22): *In each of the following questions an incomplete series of numbers, with one blank is given, identify the missing member from the given alternatives.*

19. 1, 27, 125, ...?..... 729
    A. 242
    B. 314
    C. 307
    D. 343

20. 2, 5, 10, 50, 500, ...?.....
    A. 25000
    B. 560
    C. 550
    D. 540

21. 3, 14, 47, ...?..... 443, 1334
    A. 61
    B. 89
    C. 146
    D. 445

22. 2, 9, 30, 93, 282, ...?.....
    A. 849
    B. 846
    C. 649
    D. 746

Directions (Qs. 23 to 26): *In each of the following questions there are five groups of letters. First is the primary one, followed by four; out of which one is different from the rest. Identify this odd member.*

23. IIJL
    A. QQSV
    B. EEFH
    C. AABD
    D. MMNP

24. ABAC
    A. BCBD
    B. PRPQ
    C. CDCE
    D. STSU

25. BXTP
    A. OKGC
    B. DZVR
    C. XTOK
    D. EAWS

26. DINS
    A. HMSX
    B. FKPU
    C. JOTY
    D. NSXC

27. Which pair is different in some way from others in the following pairs?
    A. Bottle and ink
    B. Can and oil
    C. Bag and clothes
    D. Boat and ship

Directions (Qs. 28 to 32): *In each of the following questions there are five figures. First is a reference figure. Among the answer figures one figure does not belong to the class to which the first figure belongs. Identify this odd figure.*

28. 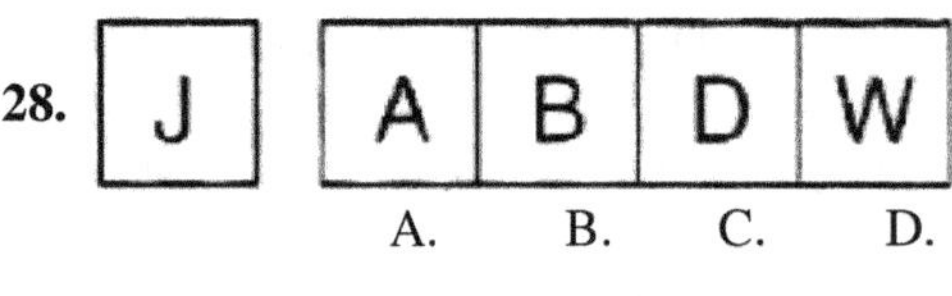

    A.   B.   C.   D.

29. 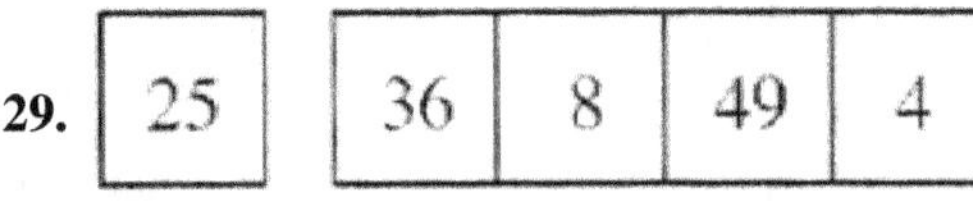

    A.   B.   C.   D.

30. 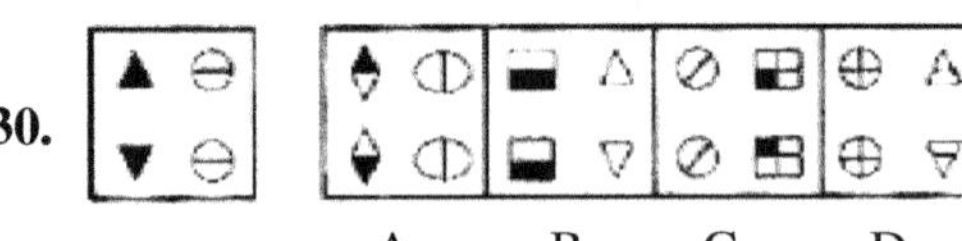
    A.   B.   C.   D.

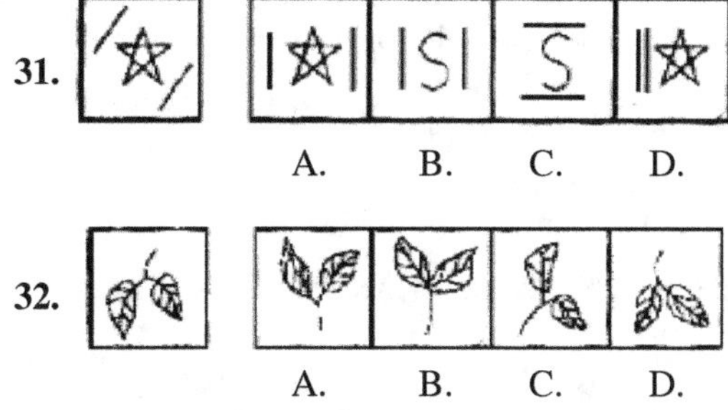

31.   A.   B.   C.   D.

32.   A.   B.   C.   D.

Directions (Qs. 33 to 36): *In each of the following questions two statements are followed by two conclusions. Assuming that the two given statements are true (however absurd they may be) decide which of the two conclusions follows strictly from the given statements. Select the most appropriate alternative.*

33. All men are chairs.
All animals are chairs.
Conclusions:
I. All men are animals.
II. No animal is a man.
A. Only I follows
B. Only II follows
C. Both I and II follow
D. Neither I nor II follows

34. Buckets are means of transport.
Stairs are means of transport.
Conclusions:
I. Buckets are stairs.
II. Some stairs are buckets.
A. Only I follows
B. Only II follows
C. Both I and II follow
D. Neither I nor II follows

35. No bird has wings.
All birds are rational.
Conclusions:
I. Some rationals have wings.
II. Wingless are birds.
A. Only I follows
B. Only II follows
C. Both I and II follow
D. Neither I nor II follows

36. All philosophers are rational people.
Some rational people are happy.
Conclusions:
I. Some happy people are philosophers.
II. Some happy people are rational.
A. Only I follows
B. Only II follows
C. Both I and II follow
D. Neither I nor II follows

37. Clothes do not dry quickly on a rainy day because on a rainy day—
A. Humidity is high
B. Humidity is low
C. Temperature becomes high
D. Atmospheric pressure rises

38. Joule is the unit of—
A. Force   B. Power
C. Energy   D. Pressure

39. The audible range of hearing for average human beings is—
A. 20 Hz to 20 KHz
B. 2 Hz to 20 Hz
C. 2 Hz to 20 KHz
D. 2 KHz to 20 KHz

40. Tritium is an—
A. Isobar of Hydrogen
B. Isotope of Hydrogen
C. Isobar of Helium
D. Isotope of Helium

41. Which of the following ions helps in the opening and closing of stomata?
A. Na^+
B. K^+
C. Ca^{++}
D. None of the above

42. Which of the following does not have plus (+) or minus (–) signs marked on it?
A. Resistor   B. Ammeter
C. Voltmeter   D. Battery

43. Photosynthesis is a—
A. Catabolic process
B. Anabolic process
C. Amphibolic process
D. All of these

44. If a mirror forms an erect but diminished image of an object placed anywhere in front of it, is a—
A. Concave Mirror
B. Plane Mirror
C. Convex Mirror
D. Concave and Convex Mirror (both)

45. The instrument to measure atmospheric pressure is called—
A. Pyrometer   B. Thermopile
C. Barometer   D. Manometer

46. Orange colour of the setting sun is due to—
A. Reflection of light
B. Diffusion of light
C. Scattering of light
D. Polarisation of light

47. What is the final colour of blue litmus when a dilute solution of NaOH is added to it?
A. Red   B. Pink
C. Orange   D. Blue

48. Pick the odd one out—
A. Fermentation
B. Aerobic Respiration
C. Anaerobic Respiration
D. Breathing

49. Hypotonic solution as compared to Hypertonic solution has—
A. More solute
B. Less solute
C. Same solute
D. Nothing can be said about the amount of solute

50. Volt is the unit of—
A. Charge
B. Current
C. Resistance
D. Potential difference

51. Two resistors having resistances of 1 ohm and 2 ohms respectively are connected in series with a battery. The current through the 2 ohms resistor is 2 amperes. The current through the 1 ohm resistor will be—
A. 0.5 amp   B. 1 amp
C. 2 amp   D. 4 amp

52. The addition of which one of the following will decrease the pH value of water?
A. Caustic Soda
B. Baking soda
C. Salt
D. Hydrochloric acid

53. The branch of science that deals with tumours is—
A. Osteology   B. Anatomy
C. Oncology   D. Urology

54. Pneumonia is a disease associated with—
A. Liver   B. Lungs
C. Gums   D. Kidney

55. The Treaty of Sreerangapattanam was between Tipu Sultan and—
A. Cornwallis   B. Clive
C. Warren Hastings   D. Wellesley

56. The famous Besnagar Pillar Inscription of century 150 BC refers to the great theistic cult of—
A. Panchika and Hariti
B. Pashupatis
C. Krishna-Vasudeva
D. Shakti

57. What is the water hyacinth?
A. A weed
B. A medicinal plant
C. A decorative plant
D. A highly sought after plant

58. To which of the following bills must the President accord his sanction without sending it back for recommendations?
A. Ordinary bills
B. Finance bills
C. Bills passed by both the houses of Parliament
D. Bills seeking amendment to the Constitution

59. The amendment procedure of the Indian Constitution has been modelled on the constitutional pattern of—
A. Canada   B. USA
C. Switzerland   D. South Africa

60. Indian Railways tied up with which of the following to launch a co-branded card and traveller loyalty card to tap the huge railway passengers market?
A. BoB cards
B. Citibank card
C. SBI card
D. None of these

61. Which bank advertises itself as the world's local bank?
A. Citibank
B. HSBC
C. ICICI Bank
D. ABN Amro

62. In which state is Silent Valley located?
A. Tamil Nadu
B. Kerala
C. Assam (Asom)
D. Arunachal Pradesh

63. Which of the following is not a promotional and motivational measure suggested in the National Population Policy 2000?
A. Reward Panchayat and Zila Parishad for promoting small family norm
B. Incentive to adopt two child norm
C. Couples below poverty line will be given health insurance plans
D. Banning abortion facilities (looking at female infanticides)

64. Who said, "HANOZ DELHI DOOR AST"?
A. Nizamuddin Aulia
B. Farid
C. Nasiruddin
D. None of these

65. In which of the following constitutional documents did the British Government for the first time, officially lay down as the goal of constitutional development in India, not only dominion status, but also responsible Government?
A. Indian Council Act, 1892
B. Indian Council Act, 1909
C. Government of India Act, 1919
D. Government of India Act, 1935

66. In which state is chromite abundantly found?
A. Maharashtra
B. Madhya Pradesh
C. Odisha
D. Karnataka

67. For what is the Manas Sanctuary in Assam known?
A. Bear
B. Tiger
C. Wild ass
D. Birds

68. The Rajya Sabha can take initiative in—
A. Censuring a Central Minister
B. Creating a new All India Service
C. Considering Money Bills
D. Appointing Judges

69. Which of the following provides the largest part of the demand for loanable funds in India?
A. Hire purchase borrowers
B. Private house purchasers
C. Corporate businesses
D. Farmers

70. Who amongst the following was impeached in England for acts committed as Governor General of India?
A. Wellesley
B. Cavendish Bentinck
C. Cornwallis
D. Warren Hastings

71. The National Stock Exchange of India (NSEI) was inaugurated in—
A. July, 1992
B. July, 1993
C. July, 1994
D. July, 1995

72. One of the major towns of the Godavari region in the Satavahana kingdom was—
A. Pratishthana
B. Arikamedu
C. Kokkhai
D. Maski

73. Anil sells a table to Kamal at a profit of 10% and Kamal sells it to Rajat at a profit of 12%. If Rajat pays ₹ 246.40 for it, then how much had Anil paid for it?
A. ₹ 220
B. ₹ 215
C. ₹ 200
D. ₹ 233

74. If the price of oranges was less by 40%, one could buy 32 more for ₹ 120. The price presently is:
A. ₹ 3.00
B. ₹ 2.00
C. ₹ 1.50
D. ₹ 2.50

75. What is the range of India's most advanced missile in the Agni series–Agni-V?
A. 2000 km
B. Over 3000 km
C. 4000 km
D. Over 5000 km

ANSWERS

1	2	3	4	5	6	7	8	9	10
B	A	C	D	D	A	B	C	B	D

11	12	13	14	15	16	17	18	19	20
A	C	C	A	B	B	C	C	D	A

21	22	23	24	25	26	27	28	29	30
C	A	A	B	C	A	D	A	B	B

31	32	33	34	35	36	37	38	39	40
D	B	D	D	B	B	A	C	A	B

41	42	43	44	45	46	47	48	49	50
B	A	C	C	C	C	D	A	B	D

51	52	53	54	55	56	57	58	59	60
C	D	C	B	A	A	A	B	D	C

61	62	63	64	65	66	67	68	69	70
B	B	D	A	C	C	B	B	C	D

71	72	73	74	75
A	A	C	D	D

EXPLANATORY ANSWERS

2. Milk in 35 litres of mixture

$$= 35 \times \frac{5}{7}$$

$$= 25 \text{ litres}$$

Water in the original mixture

$$= 35 - 25 = 10 \text{ litres}$$

Milk in new mixture $= 25 + 5 = 30$ litres

and water in new mixture $= 10$ litres

$\therefore$ Ratio of milk and water in new mixture

$$= \frac{30}{10} = \frac{3}{1}.$$

3. Let distance be x km.

Then, $\dfrac{x}{4} - \dfrac{x}{5} = \dfrac{9}{60}$

$$\Rightarrow \quad \frac{5x - 4x}{20} = \frac{9}{60}$$

$$\Rightarrow \quad 5x - 4x = \frac{9 \times 20}{60}$$

$$\Rightarrow \quad x = 3 \text{ km.}$$

5. Let the sum be ₹ x

Then,

$$\frac{x \times 4 \times 4}{100} - \frac{x \times 3 \times 5}{100} = 80$$

$$\Rightarrow \quad \frac{4x}{25} - \frac{3x}{20} = 80$$

$$\Rightarrow \quad \frac{16x - 15x}{100} = 80$$

$$\Rightarrow \quad x = ₹ \ 8000$$

6. Let $\qquad$ C.P. $= ₹ \ 100$

then, marked price $= 130$

and $\qquad$ S.P. $= 130 \times \dfrac{90}{100} = 117$

Gain $= 117 - 100 = 17$

If gain is ₹ 17 then C.P. 100

and if gain is 25.50 then

$$\frac{25.50 \times 100}{17} = ₹ \ 150.$$

7. Reduction in consumption

$$= \left(\frac{25}{125} \times 100\right)\%$$

$$= 20\%.$$

13. Let side of square $= x$ cm

then area of the square $= x^2 = 121$

$$x = 11 \ \text{cm}$$

From Question

Perimeter of the square

$$= \text{Circumference of the circle}$$

$$\Rightarrow \quad 4 \times x = 2 \ \pi \ r$$

$$(r = \text{radius of the circle})$$

$$\Rightarrow \quad 4 \times 11 = 2 \times \frac{22}{7} \times r$$

$$\Rightarrow \quad r = 7$$

$$\therefore \quad \text{Area of the circle} = \pi \times r^2$$

$$= \frac{22}{7} \times 7^2 = 154 \ \text{sq. cm.}$$

20. $2 \times 5 = 10, \ 10 \times 5 = 50,$

$50 \times 10 = 500, \ 500 \times 50 = 25000$

27. In all the rest the first is used to fill the second.

28. All the rest are consonants alike 'J' while 'A' is vowel.

29. All the rest are perfect squares.

30. In all the rest, the lower designs are the mirror image of the upper designs.

31. In all the rest, the straight lines are both sides of the middle design.

32. In all the rest both the leaves are not joined at one place.

FIRST STAGE COMPUTER BASED TEST (CBT)

1. The value of:

$$\dfrac{\sqrt{\dfrac{1+a}{1-a}}+\sqrt{\dfrac{1-a}{1+a}}}{\sqrt{\dfrac{1+a}{1-a}}-\sqrt{\dfrac{1-a}{1+a}}}-\dfrac{1}{a} \text{ is}$$

  A. 0   B. 1

  C. a D. $2 + a$

2. If $p = x + y$ and $q = x - y$, then the expression $\dfrac{p+q}{p-q}-\dfrac{p-q}{p+q}$ has a value:

  A. $\dfrac{x^2-y^2}{4xy}$ B. $\dfrac{x^2-y^2}{xy}$

  C. $\dfrac{x^2+y^2}{2xy}$ D. 0

3. One-third of a number is greater than one-fourth of its successor by one. The number is:

  A. 27   B. 39

  C. 15   D. 18

4. When the repeating decimal 0.363636 .... is written in simplest fractional form, the sum of numerator and denominator is:

  A. 135   B. 114

  C. 45   D. 15

5. A number of persons paid equal amounts and collected ₹ 72. If there were 3 persons less, then each would have to contribute ₹ 4 more. The number of people was:

  A. 12   B. 9

  C. 36   D. 6

6. A sum of ₹ 61 is divided among A, B, and C. A gets twice as much as B and C gets ₹ 5 less than A and B together. The amount that C gets is:

  A. ₹ 22

  B. ₹ 33

  C. ₹ 28

  D. ₹ 11

7. 6.4% of 2.5 is:

  A. 16   B. 1.6

  C. 0.6   D. 0.16

8. The ratio of incomes of A and B is 9 : 7. The ratio of their expenditures is 4 : 3. If each of them saves ₹ 200 per month, then the monthly income of A is:

  A. ₹ 3,600   B. ₹ 1,400

  C. ₹ 2,700   D. ₹ 1,800

9. The sum of the series 2+ 4 + 6 ... + 98 + 100 is:

  A. 2601   B. 2550

  C. 2499   D. 1545

10. If $\sin A = \dfrac{24}{25}$, the value of tan A + sec A, where $\theta° < A < 90°$ is:

  A. 7   B. 5

  C. 1   D. $\dfrac{24}{7}$

11. If the H.C.F. of the polynomials $x^3 - 3x^2 + px + 24$ and $x^2 - 7x + q$ is $(x - 2)$, the value of $(p + q)$ is:

  A. 0   B. 20

  C. −20   D. 40

12. The value of $\dfrac{3\sin 62°}{\cos 28°} - \dfrac{\sec 42°}{\operatorname{cosec} 48°}$ is:

A. 0   B. 1
C. −1   D. 2

13. Each edge of a cube is increased by 50%, the percentage increase in the surface area of the cube is:

A. 50   B. 100
C. 125   D. 200

14. The outer diameter of a spherical shell is 10 cm and the inner diameter is 8 cm. The volume of the metal contained in the shell is (Use $\pi = \dfrac{22}{7}$):

A. 255.6 cm³   B. 2044.9 cm³
C. 265.3 cm³   D. 523.8 cm³

15. Two poles of heights 7 metres and 12 metres stand on a plane ground. If the distance between their feet is 12 metres, the distance between their tops is:

A. 5 m   B. 13 m
C. 15 m   D. 20 m

16. The lengths of the diagonals of a rhombus are 24 cm and 10 cm. The side of the rhombus is:

A. 14 cm   B. 17 cm
C. 13 cm   D. 12 cm

17. The mean of 25 observations is 36. If the mean of first 13 observations is 32 and the mean of last 13 observations is 39, the 13th observation is:

A. 26   B. 25
C. 24   D. 23

18. The mid-points of the sides of a triangle ABC are (1, 1), (3, −3) and (4, 5). The coordinates of the centroid of Δ ABC are:

A. $\left(\dfrac{8}{3}, 1\right)$ B. $\left(\dfrac{8}{3}, 3\right)$

C. $\left(3, \dfrac{8}{3}\right)$ D. $\left(1, \dfrac{8}{3}\right)$

Directions (19-22): *Read the passage to answer the questions that follow.*

There is a cube with six surfaces painted Red, White, Blue, Yellow, Black and Green in such an order that Black is at the top face, Green is bottom and the other four colours are arranged in the order given in an anticlockwise direction of the surfaces. Now answer the following questions (11-14), if Red is towards you.

19. If the cube is rotated horizontally first by 180°, then rotated downwardly by 180°, then which colour would be facing downward?
A. White   B. Blue
C. Yellow   D. Black

20. If the cube is rotated clockwise (right to left) horizontally by 180° from initial position and then rotated upwardly by 90°, then which colour of the cube would be facing you?
A. Green   B. Red
C. Blue   D. Black

21. In the above question (20) which colour would be facing on the left side of you?
A. Red   B. Green
C. White   D. Yellow

22. Which colour(s) would be bounded by Yellow, Green and White?
A. Red
B. Blue
C. Red and Blue
D. Red and Yellow

Directions (23-26) : *In the following diagram, square stands for those who take tea, triangle stands for those who take coffee, circle stands for those who take cold drinks. Study the diagram carefully to answer the questions (23-26) that follow.*

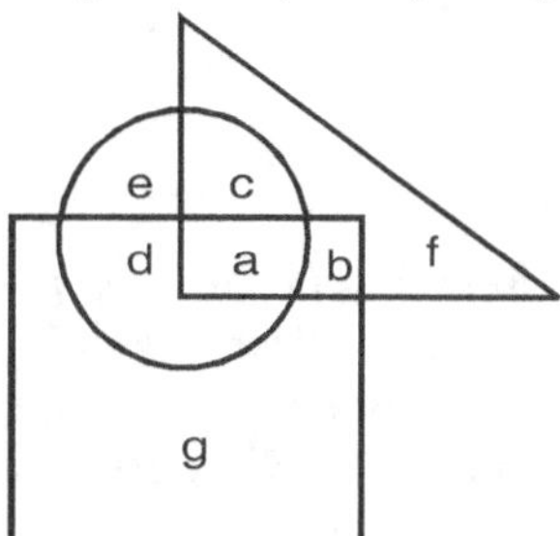

23. The persons who take tea and coffee but do not take cold drinks are represented by which letter?

A. a   B. b
C. c   D. d

24. The persons who take tea and cold drinks but do not take coffee are represented by which letter?

A. a   B. b
C. c   D. d

25. The persons who take tea, coffee and cold drinks are represented by which letter?

A. a   B. b
C. c   D. d

26. The persons who take cold drinks and coffee but do not take tea are represented by which letter?

A. a   B. b
C. c   D. d

Directions (27-30) : *In the following questions an incomplete series with one blank is given. Find out the best suited missing number from the given alternatives.*

27. 1, 4, 8, 11, 15, ?, 22
A. 19   B. 18
C. 17   D. 20

28. 1, 4, 9, 16, ?
A. 23   B. 24
C. 25   D. 30

29. 1, 3, 7, 15, 31, ?
A. 62   B. 63
C. 61   D. 71

30. 1, 2, 6, 24, ?
A. 120
B. 144
C. 30
D. 140

Directions (31-34) : *In each of the following questions there are five figures. First is a reference figure. Among the rest four figures one figure does not belong to a class to which first figure belongs. Identify this odd figure.*

Reference Figure   *Answer Figures*

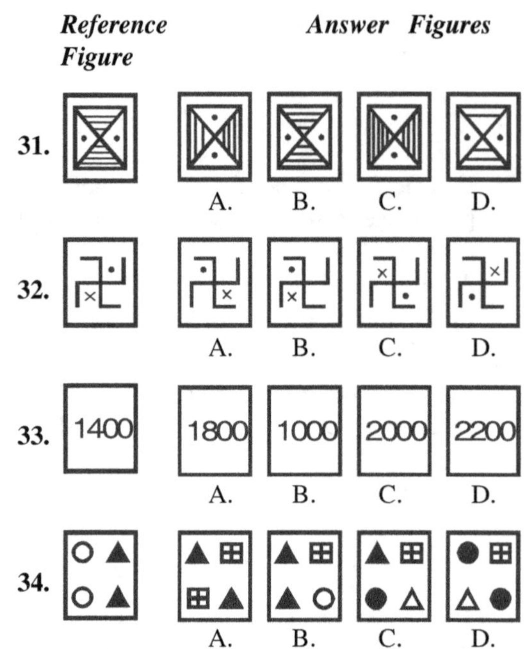

31.
       A.   B.   C.   D.

32.
       A.   B.   C.   D.

33. 1400   1800   1000   2000   2200
       A.   B.   C.   D.

34.
       A.   B.   C.   D.

Directions (35 and 36): *In each of the following questions, two statements are followed by two conclusions. Assuming the first two statements to be true (however absurd they may be), decide which of the two follows logically from the given statements. Select the most appropriate alternative from the ones given.*

35. All boys are not students.
Some students are not employed.
Conclusions:
I. Some boys are not employed.
II. Some employed ones are not boys.
A. Only I follows
B. Only II follows
C. Both I and II follow
D. Neither I nor II follows

36. All animals are dogs.
All cats are animals.
Conclusions:
I. All cats are dogs.
II. All dogs are cats.
A. Only I follows
B. Only II follows
C. Both I and II follow
D. Neither I nor II follows

37. Which of the following colours has the shortest wavelength?
A. Red
B. Orange
C. Yellow
D. Violet

38. In a diesel engine, the fuel is ignited by:
A. a spark plug
B. liquid oxygen
C. the heat generated when air is compressed in the cylinder
D. vaporization under partial vacuum

39. How many moons does the Pluto have?
A. None
B. One
C. Two
D. Six

40. The weight of a body on the moon is:
A. 1/5th of its weight on earth
B. 1/6th of its weight on earth
C. 1/7th of its weight on earth
D. 1/100th of its weight on earth

41. The scientific study of the action of chemicals upon living beings is called:
A. Pharmacy
B. Pharmacognosy
C. Pharmacology
D. Biochemistry

42. In the manufacturing of match stick, which of the following is used?
A. Potassium
B. Sodium
C. White phosphorous
D. Red phosphorous

43. What did Fleming discover?
A. Vitamin A
B. Vaccines
C. Sulphonamides
D. Penicillin

44. The substance present inside a fluorescent tube which emits light is:
A. Nitrogen
B. Mercury vapour
C. Sodium cyanide
D. Air

45. The biological process by which changes occur in genes is known as:
A. Adaptation
B. Evolution
C. Natural selection
D. Mutation

46. Agronomy is the study of:
A. behaviour of agricultural animals
B. field crop production and soils
C. names of agricultural plants
D. all of these

47. Cold-blooded animals are those animals whose:
A. blood is cold
B. blood is blue, not red
C. body temperature varies with that of the surroundings
D. body temperature is always constant

48. What is the technical term for fish farming?
A. Aviculture
B. Sericulture
C. Pisciculture
D. Zooculutre

49. The vision defect of eyes as a result of which a person is unable to see distant objects clearly, is called:
A. Hypermetropia
B. Long sightedness
C. Astigmatism
D. Myopia

50. Which of the following diseases is caused by amoeba?
A. Paralysis
B. Cholera
C. Dysentery
D. Typhoid fever

51. The wind blowing from the land towards the sea during the night is known as:
A. Ordinary breeze
B. Sea breeze
C. Land breeze
D. Cold breeze

52. Dots are placed on dice in such a fashion that the sum of dots on any two opposite sides is always:
A. 9
B. 7
C. 6
D. 8

53. If the earth did not spin:
A. we would have no seasons
B. half of earth would always be in sunlight
C. there would be no summer in the northern hemisphere
D. all of the above

54. The most abundant element in the earth's crust is:
A. Oxygen
B. Silicon
C. Aluminium
D. Iron

55. What is the rank of India in the 2004 Index of Economic Freedom, published by the Heritage Foundation and the Wall Street Journal?
A. 84
B. 71
C. 121
D. 90

56. Who was the Governor-General when the 1857 revolt broke out?
A. Dalhousie
B. Canning
C. Curzon
D. Lawrence

57. The Twelfth Finance Commission has recommended to bring down the revenue deficit of the Centre and the State to zero by
A. 2005-2006
B. 2006-2007
C. 2007-2008
D. 2008-2009

58. In Union Budget 2005, the finance minister introduced a new tax called FBT. What is the full name of the term FBT?
A. Fiscal Benefit Tax
B. Fringe Benefit Tax
C. Fixed Benefit Tax
D. None of these

59. Fawazil was
A. extra payment made to the nobles
B. excess amount paid to the Exchequer by the Iqtedar
C. revenue assigned in lieu of salary
D. none of these

60. Which one of the following is *not* a statutory body?
A. The Election Commission
B. The Union Public Service Commission
C. The Planning Commission
D. The Finance Commission

61. Which of the following countries is *not* a member of Mercosur?
A. Brazil
B. Paraguay
C. Peru
D. Chile

62. Which theory makes the use of Jigsaw fit in its support?
A. Tidal Hypothesis
B. Tetrahydral Hypothesis
C. Cycle of Erosion
D. Continental Drift Theory

63. Where is the famous Tuscarora dweep located?
A. Near USA
B. Off Japan
C. Off Lakshadweep
D. Near the Australian coast

64. In which of the following countries has there been the highest rise in overall level of skilled unemployed during 2000-2002?
A. India
B. China
C. France
D. USA

65. The Rigveda consists of
A. 1028 hymns
B. 1000 hymns
C. 2028 hymns
D. 1038 hymns

66. Blizzards are characteristic of .... region.
A. Equatorial
B. Tropical
C. Antarctic
D. Temperate

67. Which of the following Harappan sites are located in Uttar Pradesh?
A. Kalibangan
B. Banawali
C. Alamgirpur
D. Sutkagen-dor

68. The Prime Minister Manmohan Singh has constituted a task force to prepare a long term plan for the social and economic development of:
A. Tamil Nadu
B. Manipur
C. Jammu and Kashmir
D. Uttarakhand

69. How many islands make up Hong Kong?
A. 235
B. 245
C. 205
D. 206

70. Commonwealth Bank belongs to which country?
A. Australia
B. New Zealand
C. United Kingdom
D. Philippines

71. What does NIFE refer to?
A. A crop
B. An instrument
C. A marine organism
D. A type of rock

72. Who started the Madras Labour Union in 1918?
   A. Kanji Dwarkadas and Umar Sobhani
   B. G. Ramanjulu Naidu and G.C. Chetti
   C. T.K. Murlidhar and H.B. Mahaduvle
   D. C.K. Annadurai and K.T. Ramchandar

73. *INS Karanj*, which was launched on January 31, 2018 in Mumbai is India's .... Scorpene class submarine.
   A. 1st   B. 4th
   C. 2nd   D. 3rd

74. What is Pratyush?
   A. India's fastest supercomputer
   B. India's navigational satellite
   C. Shape-changing cell-sized Robot
   D. WHO nodded Indian typhoid vaccine

75. Scientists in which country have created the first monkeys cloned by the same process that produced Dolly the sheep more than 20 years ago?
   A. USA   B. South Korea
   C. China   D. India

ANSWERS

1	2	3	4	5	6	7	8	9	10
A	B	C	D	B	C	D	D	B	A
11	12	13	14	15	16	17	18	19	20
A	D	C	A	B	C	D	A	D	A
21	22	23	24	25	26	27	28	29	30
C	C	B	D	A	C	B	C	B	A
31	32	33	34	35	36	37	38	39	40
D	B	C	C	A	A	D	A	A	B
41	42	43	44	45	46	47	48	49	50
C	D	D	A	D	B	C	C	D	C
51	52	53	54	55	56	57	58	59	60
C	B	D	C	C	D	D	D	B	C
61	62	63	64	65	66	67	68	69	70
B	A	B	A	A	A	C	B	A	A
71	72	73	74	75					
A	C	D	A	C					

EXPLANATORY ANSWERS

1.
$$\dfrac{\sqrt{\dfrac{1+a}{1-a}} + \sqrt{\dfrac{1-a}{1+a}}}{\sqrt{\dfrac{1+a}{1-a}} - \sqrt{\dfrac{1-a}{1+a}}} - \dfrac{1}{a}$$

$$= \dfrac{1+a+1-a}{1+a-1+a} - \dfrac{1}{a}$$

$$= \dfrac{2}{2a} - \dfrac{1}{a} = 0$$

2. $\because p = x + y$ and $q = x - y$

$$\therefore \dfrac{p+q}{p-q} - \dfrac{p-q}{p+q}$$

$$= \dfrac{(p^2 + 2pq + q^2) - (p^2 - 2pq + q^2)}{p^2 - q^2}$$

$$= \dfrac{4pq}{p^2 - q^2}$$

$$= \frac{4(x+y)(x-y)}{(x+y)^2 - (x-y)^2}$$

$$= \frac{4(x^2 - y^2)}{x^2 + 2xy + y^2 - x^2 + 2xy - y^2}$$

$$= \frac{x^2 - y^2}{xy}$$

3. Let the number be x and the successor is $x + 1$

ATQ, $\dfrac{1}{3}x - \dfrac{1}{4}(x + 1) = 1$

$\Rightarrow 4x - 3x - 3 = 12$

$\Rightarrow x = 15$

4. Suppose $x = 0.363636 \ldots.$ ...(*i*)

Multiplying both sides of (*i*) by 100,

$\qquad 100\,x = 36.363636\ldots.$ ...(*ii*)

Subtracting (*i*) from (*ii*), we get

$\qquad 99x = 36$

$\therefore \qquad x = \dfrac{36}{99} = \dfrac{4}{11}$

Thus, the sum of numerator and denominator

of $\dfrac{4}{11}$ is 15.

5. Let the number of people be x.

As per the given condition,

$$\frac{72}{x - 3} - \frac{72}{x} = 4$$

$$\Rightarrow \frac{72[x - x + 3]}{x(x - 3)} = 4$$

$$\Rightarrow 4(x^2 - 3x) = 72 \times 3$$

$$\Rightarrow x^2 - 3x - 54 = 0$$

$$\Rightarrow x(x - 9) + 6(x - 9) = 0$$

Either $x + 6 = 0$ or $x - 9 = 0$

$x = -6$ (not possible) $x = 9$

6. Let the amount of B be ₹ x

so that the amount of A = ₹ $2x$

The amount of C = ₹ $(3x - 5)$

ATQ, $\quad x + 2x + (3x - 5) = 61$

$\Rightarrow \qquad\qquad 6x = 66$

$\therefore \qquad\qquad x = 11$

Thus, the amount that "C" gets

$\qquad\qquad = 3 \times 11 - 5$

$\qquad\qquad = ₹ \, 28$

7. 6.4% of 2.5 $= \dfrac{6.4}{100} \times 2.5$

$$= \frac{64}{1000} \times \frac{25}{10}$$

$$= 0.16$$

8. Let the income of A = ₹ $9x$

and the income of B = ₹ $7x$

Also, the expenditure of A = ₹ $4y$

and the expenditure of B = ₹ $3y$

As per the condition,

$\qquad\qquad 9x - 4y = 200$ ...(*i*)

And $\qquad\quad 7x - 3y = 200$ ...(*ii*)

Solving eqn. (*i*) and (*ii*) we get

$\qquad\qquad x = 200$

So, $\qquad$ income of A $= 9 \times 200$

$\qquad\qquad\qquad = ₹ \, 1800$

9. Here, $a = 2$

$$d = 4 - 2 = 2$$

$$t_n = a + (n - 1)d$$

$\Rightarrow \qquad 100 = 2 + (n - 1) \times 2$

$\Rightarrow \qquad 100 = 2 + 2n - 2$

$\therefore \qquad n = \dfrac{100}{2} = 50$

$\therefore \qquad S_n = \dfrac{n}{2}\{2a + (n - 1) \times d\}$

$$S_{50} = \frac{50}{2}\{2 \times 2 + (50 - 1) \times 2\}$$

$$= 25(4 + 49 \times 2)$$

$$= 25 \times 102$$

$$= 2550.$$

10. $\because \sin A = \dfrac{24}{25}$

$$\cos A = \sqrt{1 - \sin^2 A} = \sqrt{1 - \left(\dfrac{24}{25}\right)^2}$$

$$= \sqrt{1 - \dfrac{576}{625}} = \sqrt{\dfrac{625 - 576}{625}}$$

$$= \sqrt{\dfrac{49}{625}} = \dfrac{7}{25}$$

$\therefore$ The value of $\tan A + \sec A$

$$= \dfrac{\sin A}{\cos A} + \dfrac{1}{\cos A}$$

$$= \dfrac{1 + \sin A}{\cos A}$$

$$= \dfrac{1 + \dfrac{24}{25}}{\dfrac{7}{25}} = \dfrac{\dfrac{49}{25}}{\dfrac{7}{25}} = \dfrac{49}{7} = 7$$

11. Since, HCF of the polynomials

$x^3 - 3x^2 + px + 24$ and $x^2 - 7x + q$ is $x - 2$

Here we put $x = 2$ in the given polynomials, we have

$(2)^3 - 3 \times 2^2 + p \times 2 + 24 = 0$

$\Rightarrow \qquad 8 - 12 + 2p + 24 = 0$

$\qquad\qquad\qquad 2p = -20$

$\therefore \qquad\qquad\qquad p = -10$

Again, $\quad (2)^2 - 7 \times 2 + q = 0$

$\Rightarrow \qquad\qquad 4 - 14 + q = 0$

$\Rightarrow \qquad\qquad -10 + q = 0$

$\therefore \qquad\qquad\qquad q = 10$

$\therefore \qquad\qquad p + q = -10 + 10 = 0$

12. $\dfrac{3 \sin 62°}{\cos 28°} - \dfrac{\sec 42°}{\cos 48°}$

$$= \dfrac{3\sin(90° - 28°)}{\cos 28°} - \dfrac{\sec 42°}{\operatorname{cosec}(90 - 42°)}$$

$$= \dfrac{3 \cos 28°}{\cos 28°} - \dfrac{\sec 42°}{\sec 42°}$$

$$= 3 - 1 = 2.$$

13. Suppose each edge of the cube be x, on increasing 50% of each edge,

$$\text{New edge} = x + \dfrac{1}{2}x = \dfrac{3x}{2}$$

Original surface area of the cube $= 6l^2$

$$= 6x^2$$

New surface area of the cube

$$= 6\left(\dfrac{3x}{2}\right)^2$$

$$= 6 \times \dfrac{9x^2}{4}$$

$$= \dfrac{27}{2}x^2$$

Increase in surface area

$$= \dfrac{27}{2}x^2 - 6x^2$$

$$= \dfrac{27x^2 - 12x^2}{2}$$

$$= \dfrac{15x^2}{2}$$

$\therefore$ % increase $= \dfrac{\dfrac{15x^2}{2}}{6x^2} \times 100 = 125$

14. The volume of the metal contained in the shell

$$= \dfrac{4}{3}\pi\,(R^3 - r^3)$$

Here $R = 5$, $r = 4$

$\therefore \qquad V = \dfrac{4}{3}\pi\left[(5)^3 - (4)^3\right]$

$$= \dfrac{4}{3} \times \dfrac{22}{7}\,[125 - 64]$$

$$= \dfrac{4}{3} \times \dfrac{22}{7} \times 61$$

$$= 255.619 \approx 255.62 \text{ cm}^3$$

15.

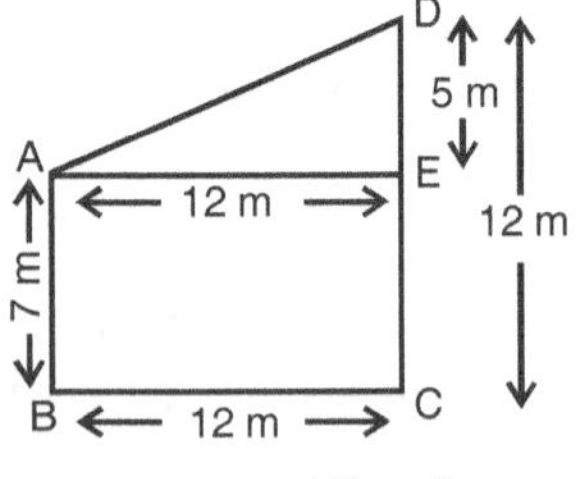

$$AB = 7 \text{ m}$$
$$CD = 12 \text{ m}$$
$$BC = AE = 12 \text{ m}$$
$$DE = CD - CE$$
$$= CD - AB$$
$$= 12 - 7 = 5 \text{ m}$$
$$AD^2 = AE^2 + DE^2$$
$$= (12)^2 + (5)^2$$
$$= 144 + 25 = 169$$
$$\therefore \quad AD = \sqrt{169} = 13 \text{ m}$$

16.
$$d_1 = 24 \text{ cm}$$
$$d_2 = 10 \text{ cm}$$

Sides of the rhombus

$$= \frac{1}{2}\sqrt{d_1^2 + d_2^2}$$

$$= \frac{1}{2}\sqrt{(24)^2 + (10)^2}$$

$$= \frac{1}{2}\sqrt{576 + 100} = \frac{1}{2}\sqrt{676}$$

$$= \frac{1}{2} \times 26 = 13 \text{ cm}$$

17. Sum of 25 observations = $25 \times 36 = 900$

Sum of first 13 observations
$$= 13 \times 32 = 416$$

Sum of last 13 observations
$$= 13 \times 39 = 507$$

Thus, the 13th observation
$$= 416 + 507 - 900$$
$$= 923 - 900 = 23$$

18. $\dfrac{x_1 + x_2}{2} = 1 \implies x_1 + x_2 = 2 \qquad \ldots(i)$

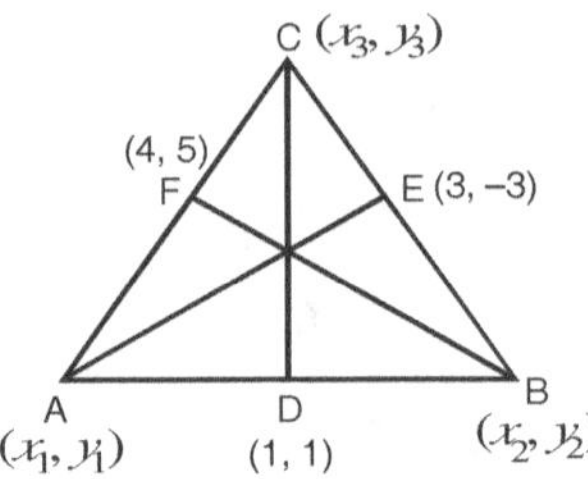

$$\frac{y_1 + y_2}{2} = 1$$
$$\implies \quad y_1 + y_2 = 2 \qquad \ldots(ii)$$

$$\frac{x_2 + x_3}{2} = 3$$
$$\implies \quad x_2 + x_3 = 6 \qquad \ldots(iii)$$

$$\frac{y_2 + y_3}{2} = -3$$
$$\implies \quad y_2 + y_3 = -6 \qquad \ldots(iv)$$

$$\frac{x_3 + x_1}{2} = 4$$
$$\implies \quad x_1 + x_3 = 8 \qquad \ldots(v)$$

$$\frac{y_3 + y_1}{2} = 5$$
$$\implies \quad y_1 + y_3 = 10 \qquad \ldots(vi)$$

Adding (i), (iii), (v), we get
$$2(x_1 + x_2 + x_3) = 16$$
$$\therefore \quad x_1 + x_2 + x_3 = 8$$
$$\therefore \quad \frac{x_1 + x_2 + x_3}{3} = \frac{8}{3}$$

Similarly, adding (ii), (iv) and (vi)
$$2(y_1 + y_2 + y_3) = 6$$
$$\therefore \quad y_1 + y_2 + y_3 = 3$$
$$\therefore \quad \frac{y_1 + y_2 + y_3}{3} = \frac{3}{3} = 1$$

Hence, the co-ordinates of centroid is $\left(\dfrac{8}{3}, 1\right)$.

RRB—Railway Recruitment Board
Assistant Loco Pilot (ALP) & Technicians,
Recruitment Examination

FIRST STAGE COMPUTER BASED TEST (CBT)

1. The value of

$$\left(a^{x-y}\right)^{x+y}\cdot\left(a^{y-z}\right)^{y+z}\cdot\left(a^{z-x}\right)^{z+x}$$ is

A. 0
B. 1
C. −1
D. $x + y + z$

2. If $A = x - \dfrac{1}{x}$, then the value of $A - \dfrac{1}{A}$ is

A. $\dfrac{2}{x}$
B. $\dfrac{2x^2 - 1}{x}$
C. $\dfrac{x^4 + 1 - x^2}{x\left(x^2 - 1\right)}$
D. $\dfrac{x^4 - 3x^2 + 1}{x\left(x^2 - 1\right)}$

3. Two numbers are in the ratio 3 : 4. If the sum of their squares is 900, the smaller number is
A. 18
B. 24
C. 16
D. 27

4. If 4 men or 6 boys can do a piece of work in 20 days, then 12 men and 2 boys will do the same work in
A. 10 days
B. 8 days
C. 6 days
D. 5 days

5. The difference between simple interest and compound interest on a sum at 5% in 2 years is ₹ 2.50. The sum is
A. ₹ 2,500
B. ₹ 2,000
C. ₹ 1,000
D. ₹ 1,500

6. The value of sin 60° cos 30° + cos 60° sin 30° is
A. 0
B. 1
C. $\dfrac{1}{2}$
D. $\dfrac{\sqrt{3}}{2}$

7. If I had walked 1km/hour faster I would have taken 10 minutes less to walk a distance of 2 km. The rate of my walking is
A. 4 km/hour
B. 3 km/hour
C. 6 km/hour
D. 3.5 km/hour

8. The radius of a semicircular disc is 10.5 cm. The perimeter of the disc is
A. 33 cm
B. 21 cm
C. 44 cm
D. 54 cm

9. Three consecutive vertices of a parallelogram are A (1, 2), B(1, 0) and C (4, 0). The fourth vertex D is
A. $\left(\dfrac{5}{2}, 1\right)$
B. (2, 1)
C. (4, 2)
D. (2, 4)

10. One year ago, a man was 8 times as old as his son. Now his age is equal to the square of his son's age. The present age of the son is
A. 5 years
B. 6 years
C. 7 years
D. 8 years

11. PT is a tangent to a circle from an exterior point P and PAB is a secant intersecting the circle at A and B such that PA = 3 cm and PT = 6 cm. The measure of PB is
A. 9 cm
B. 10 cm
C. 12 cm
D. 8 cm

12. A bag contains 4 red, 5 black and 6 white balls. A ball is drawn at random. The probability that the ball drawn is red or white is
A. $\dfrac{2}{5}$
B. $\dfrac{4}{15}$
C. $\dfrac{1}{3}$
D. $\dfrac{2}{3}$

(1958) Practice Papers—9

13. If 4 times the fourth term of an AP is equal to 7 times the 1st term, then the ratio of 1st term to the common difference is
A. 4 : 1
B. 1 : 4
C. 2 : 3
D. 3 : 2

14. The circumference of the base of a 9 m high cone is 44 m. The volume of the cone is
A. 1386 m^3 B. 198 m^3
C. 154 m^3 D. 462 m^3

15. The mode for the series 2, 3, 2, 5, 6, 3, 4, 7, 4, 9 is
A. 4.5   B. 4
C. 3   D. 3.5

16. The HCF of $x^2 + x - (2k + 2)$ and $2x^2 + kx - 12$ is $x + 4$. The value of k is
A. 0   B. 1
C. 2   D. 4

17. If $\sec \theta + \tan \theta = a$, then $\dfrac{a^2 - 1}{a^2 + 1}$ is equal to
A. $\sin \theta$ B. $\cos \theta$
C. $\csc \theta$ D. $\cot \theta$

18. The area of a square that can be inscribed in a circle of radius r is
A. πr^2 B. $\sqrt{2}\, r^2$
C. $4r^2$ D. $2r^2$

Directions (Qs. No. 19-23): *In the following questions a series of numbers or alphabets (of English language) is being given. You have to identify the missing number or alphabet which bears the same relation with others.*

19. 1, 3, 9, ?, 81
A. 12   B. 15
C. 27   D. 25

20. A, E, ?, O, U
A. F   B. I
C. G   D. L

21. 1, 2, 6, 24, 120, ?
A. 144   B. 480
C. 600   D. 720

22. 37, 47, 58, ?, 79, 89
A. 67   B. 68
C. 69   D. 71

23. 1221, 2442, 3663, 4884, ?
A. 5885   B. 6105
C. 6006   D. 8448

Directions (Qs. No. 24-28): *In the following questions, find the term from the given alternatives for the missing place marked?*

24. LUNCH : OWQEK : DINNER : ?
A. HJPOIS   B. HKPPIT
C. GKQPHT   D. GKPOHT

25. AUTHENTIC : AVTIEOTJC : : GENUINE : ?
A. GFNUIPE   B. GFNVIOE
C. GFNVJOE   D. GFVNOJE

26. ODOUR : ? : : SMELL : PPBOI
A. LGLXO   B. LGKXP
C. LALIO   D. LGMYP

27. COMMERCE : FSRSLZLO : : BEGIN : ?
A. EHKNU   B. EIMOV
C. EIKNU   D. EILOU

28. TREASON : ? : : REWARD : UHZDUG
A. WUGCURQ
B. WUHDWRQ
C. WUHDVRQ
D. WGHDVRQ

Directions (Qs. No. 29-33): *In each of the following questions, two statements are followed by two conclusions. Assuming the first two statements to be true, (however absurd it may be) decide which of the two logically follows strictly from the given statements. Select the most appropriate alternative from the ones given.*

29. All apples are fruits.
No fruit is vegetable.
Conclusions:
I. All apples are vegetables.
II. All fruits are apples.
A. Only I follows
B. Only II follows
C. Both I and II follow
D. Neither I nor II follows

30. All watches are machines.
All machines are living beings.
Conclusions:
I. All machines are watches.
II. All watches are living beings.
A. Only I follows
B. Only II follows
C. Both I and II follow
D. Neither I nor II follows

31. Some birds are dolls.
All animals are dolls.
Conclusions:
I. All birds are dolls.
II. Some animals are dolls.
A. Only I follows
B. Only II follows
C. Both I and II follow
D. Neither I nor II follows

32. All lenses are mirrors.
All mirrors are brushes.
Conclusions:
I. All lenses are brushes.
II. All brushes are lenses.
A. Only I follows
B. Only II follows
C. Both I and II follow
D. Neither I nor II follows

33. All animals are not birds.
Some animals are vertebrates.
Conclusions:
I. All birds are vertebrates.
II. Some birds are animals.
A. Only I follows
B. Only II follows
C. Both I and II follow
D. Neither I nor II follows

Directions (Qs. No. 34-36): *In the following questions three figures resemble each other, you have to identify the odd one.*

34.    
A.   B.   C.   D.

35. 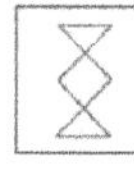  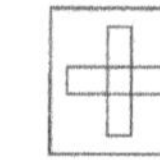
A.   B.   C.   D.

36. 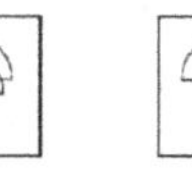 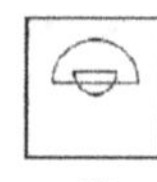
A.   B.   C.   D.

37. Which of the following are *not* electro-magnetic waves?
A. Infrared waves
B. Laser waves
C. Ultrasonic waves
D. Microwaves

38. Domestic electric meters record the consumption of electricity in
A. Volts
B. Amperes
C. Watts
D. Ohms

39. Which of the following is used for time keeping in an atomic clock?
A. Cesium
B. Helium
C. Plutonium
D. Nitrogen

40. When an aeroplane takes off, air pressure on the
A. top surface of its wings is less than the air pressure on the bottom surface
B. top surface of its wings is more than the air pressure on the bottom surface
C. top and bottom surfaces of its wings is exactly equal
D. wings is zero

41. The pH value of pure water is
A. 7
B. 0
C. 14
D. –1.0

42. The substance which readily hardens, when mixed with water is
A. Plaster of Paris
B. Granite
C. Lime
D. Silica

43. The gas commonly used for cooling in a domestic refrigerator is
A. Carbon monoxide
B. Propane and butane mixture
C. Helium
D. Neon

44. Stainless steel is basically formed by the combination of iron and
A. Chromium   B. Carbon
C. Manganese   D. Cobalt

45. The tube which connects the mouth to the stomach is known as
A. oesophagus   B. trachea
C. larynx   D. intestine

46. DNA molecules have the shape of
A. a string of beads
B. a double helix
C. a cylindrical mass
D. None of the above

47. Which portion of the egg contains cholesterol?
A. Egg white
B. Shell of the egg
C. Egg yolk
D. All parts equally

48. Aspirin is the common name of
A. salicylic acid
B. salicylate
C. acetyl salicylic acid
D. methyl salicylate

49. During galvanization, the substance which is coated on the surface of iron to protect it from rusting is
A. galium   B. aluminium
C. tin   D. zinc

50. The intensity of earthquakes is measured by
A. Algal scale
B. Crescograph
C. Ritcher scale
D. Cryptograph

51. Solar eclipse occurs when
A. earth comes between sun and moon
B. moon is at right angle to the earth
C. moon comes between sun and earth
D. sun comes between moon and earth

52. Which of the following are fossil fuels?
A. Coal and biogas
B. Petroleum and biogas
C. Biogas and coal gas
D. Coal, petroleum and natural gas

53. Clouds of intersteller matter found in space is known as
A. galaxies   B. constellations
C. quasars   D. nebula

54. The mass of a material divided by its volume is its
A. gravity   B. relative density
C. specific gravity   D. density

55. What is the name of the man who discovered that the Monsoon winds blow regularly across the Arabian Sea in summer?
A. Ptolemy   B. Hippalus
C. Pliny   D. Megasthenes

56. Who is remembered as the pioneer of Economic Nationalism?
A. Bipin Chandar Paul
B. Gokhale
C. R.C. Dutt
D. Madan Mohan Malviya

57. In the Allahabad district in 1929, at a time of the world-wide economic depression, 'no tax' campaign on behalf of peasants was led by
A. Jawahar Lal Nehru
B. Sahajanand Saraswati
C. M.N. Roy
D. P.C. Joshi

58. 'My own belief is that the Congress is tottering, and one of my great ambition is to assist it to a peaceful death.' Who said it?
A. Winston Churchill
B. Lord Canning
C. Lord Curzon
D. Mohammad Ali Jinnah

59. Aurangzeb was a scholar of
A. Poetry
B. Muslim theology and jurisprudence
C. Persian literature
D. Persian warfare

60. Who is connected with the 'Blue Water' Policy?
A. Albuquerque
B. Dupleix
C. De Almeida
D. Robert Clive

61. Who was called the 'Rapheal of the East'?
A. Bihzad of Herat
B. Sayyad Ali
C. Khwaja Abdus Samad
D. Farrukh Beg

62. Fiscal policy is connected with
A. Exports and imports
B. Public revenue and expenditure
C. Issue of currency
D. Population control

63. The expression 'The Union of States' used in the Constitution has been taken from the Constitution of
A. Canada
B. USA
C. USSR
D. Germany

64. Which one of the following statements correctly describes 'a hung Parliament'?
A. A Parliament in which no party has a clear majority
B. The Prime Minister has resigned but the Parliament is not dissolved
C. The Parliament lacks the quorum to conduct business
D. A lame duck Parliament

65. For what is Philadelphia well known?
A. Ship building
B. Dairy industries
C. Locomotives
D. Silk textiles

66. Which state is the leading producer of thorium?
A. Kerala
B. Bihar
C. Odisha
D. Madhya Pradesh

67. Who are believed to be the oldest inhabitants of India?
A. Mediterraneans
B. Negritoes
C. Nordics
D. Mongoloids

68. Most of the precipitation in India is
A. Cyclonic
B. Convectional
C. Orographic
D. Stormy

69. Who put forth the nebular hypothesis explaining the origin of the earth?
A. Wegener
B. Laplace
C. Kant
D. Jeans and Jeffreys

70. Leeds is well known for
A. Cotton textiles
B. Iron smelting
C. Films
D. Woollen textiles

71. The plan holiday refers to the period
A. 1965-68
B. 1966-69
C. 1967-70
D. 1978-80

72. Which of the following is the Indian contribution to Parliamentary procedures?
A. Zero session
B. Cut-motion
C. Adjournment motion
D. Guillotine

73. If in a code language 'MUSIC' is written as 'XVQYW' and 'USAGE' is written as 'VQZIF', then how can 'MAGIC' be written in that code:
A. XZIWY   B. XZWIY
C. XZIYW   D. XZYIW

74. If 'MEDICAL' is written as 'DEMILAC' how is 'SUBJECT' written is that code?
A. BUSJETC
B. BUSTCTE
C. BUSJTCE
D. BUJSCTE

75. If '+' means '−', '−' means '×', '×' means '÷' and '÷' means '+', then 2 ÷ 6 × 6 ÷ 2 = ?
A. 0   B. 4
C. 5   D. 10

ANSWERS

1	2	3	4	5	6	7	8	9	10
B	D	A	C	C	B	B	D	C	C

11	12	13	14	15	16	17	18	19	20
C	A	A	D	A	B	A	D	C	B

21	22	23	24	25	26	27	28	29	30
D	B	B	C	B	A	D	C	D	B

31	32	33	34	35	36	37	38	39	40
D	A	B	B	A	C	C	C	A	A

41	42	43	44	45	46	47	48	49	50
A	A	D	A	A	B	C	C	D	C

51	52	53	54	55	56	57	58	59	60
C	D	D	D	B	C	B	C	B	A

61	62	63	64	65	66	67	68	69	70
A	B	A	A	A	B	B	C	B	D

71	72	73	74	75
B	A	C	C	C

EXPLANATORY ANSWERS

1. $a^{(x-y)(x+y)} \cdot a^{(y-z)(y+z)} \cdot a^{(z-x)(z+x)}$

$a^{x^2-y^2} \cdot a^{y^2-z^2} \cdot a^{z^2-x^2}$

$a^{(x^2-y^2)+(y^2-z^2)+(z^2-x^2)}$

$a^0 = 1$

2. $A = x - \dfrac{1}{x}$

$A - \dfrac{1}{A} = \left(x - \dfrac{1}{x}\right) - \dfrac{1}{\left(x - \dfrac{1}{x}\right)}$

$= \dfrac{\left(x - \dfrac{1}{x}\right)^2 - 1}{x - \dfrac{1}{x}} = \dfrac{\left(x^2 - 2 + \dfrac{1}{x^2}\right) - 1}{x - \dfrac{1}{x}}$

$= \dfrac{x^2 + \dfrac{1}{x^2} - 3}{\dfrac{x^2 - 1}{x}} = \dfrac{\dfrac{x^4 + 1 - 3x^2}{x^2}}{\dfrac{x^2 - 1}{x}}$

$= \dfrac{x^4 + 1 - 3x^2}{x^2} \cdot \dfrac{x}{x^2 - 1} = \dfrac{x^4 - 3x^2 + 1}{x(x^2 - 1)}$

3. $\dfrac{x}{y} = \dfrac{3}{4}$ $\qquad \therefore x = \dfrac{3y}{4}$

$x^2 + y^2 = 900$

$\left(\dfrac{3y}{4}\right)^2 + y^2 = 900$

$\dfrac{9y^2}{16} + y^2 = 900$

$25y^2 = 900 \times 16$

or $\qquad y^2 = \dfrac{900 \times 16}{25}$

or $\qquad y = \sqrt{\dfrac{900 \times 16}{25}}$

$= \dfrac{30 \times 4}{5} = 24$

$x = \dfrac{3 \times 24}{4} = 18$

4.
$$4M = 6B$$

$$1M = \frac{6}{4}B$$

$$12M = \frac{6}{4} \times 12 = 18B$$

12 Men + 2 Boys = 18 Boys + 2 Boys
$$= 20 \text{ Boys}$$

∵ 6 Boys are doing a work in 20 days

∴ 1 Boy is doing a work in 20 × 6 days

∴ 20 Boys are doing a work in $\dfrac{20 \times 6}{20} = 6$ days

5.
$$\left[x\left(1+\frac{5}{100}\right)^2 - x\right] - \frac{x \cdot 5 \cdot 2}{100} = 2.50$$

$$\Rightarrow \left[x\left(\frac{21}{20}\right)^2 - x\right] - \frac{x}{10} = 2.50$$

$$\Rightarrow \left[\frac{441x}{400} - x\right] - \frac{x}{10} = 2.50$$

$$\Rightarrow \frac{441x - 400x}{400} - \frac{x}{10} = 2.50$$

$$\Rightarrow \frac{41x}{400} - \frac{x}{10} = 2.50$$

$$\Rightarrow \frac{41x - 40x}{400} = 2.50$$

or $\qquad x = 2.50 \times 400 = ₹\ 1000$

6. $\sin 60° \cos 30° + \cos 60° \sin 30°$

$$\frac{\sqrt{3}}{2} \cdot \frac{\sqrt{3}}{2} + \frac{1}{2} \cdot \frac{1}{2} = \frac{3}{4} + \frac{1}{4}$$

$$= \frac{3+1}{4} = \frac{4}{4} = 1$$

7. Suppose Speed = x km/h

time taken, $\qquad t_1 = \dfrac{\text{distance}}{\text{speed}} = \dfrac{2}{x} h$

if Speed = $(x + 1)$ km/h

then time = $t_2 = \dfrac{2}{x+1} h \qquad \ldots(i)$

but according to question,

time, $\qquad t_2 = \left(\dfrac{2}{x} - \dfrac{10}{60}\right) h \qquad \ldots(ii)$

From eq. (i) and (ii)

$$\frac{2}{x+1} = \frac{2}{x} - \frac{1}{6}$$

$$\frac{2}{x} - \frac{2}{x+1} = \frac{1}{6}$$

$$\frac{2x + 2 - 2x}{x(x+1)} = \frac{1}{6}$$

or $\qquad \dfrac{2}{x(x+1)} = \dfrac{1}{6}$

or $\qquad x^2 + x = 12$

or $\qquad x^2 + x - 12 = 0$

or $\qquad x^2 + 4x - 3x - 12 = 0$

or $\quad x(x + 4) - 3(x + 4) = 0$

$\qquad (x - 3)(x + 4) = 0$

∴ $\qquad\qquad x = 3$ km/h

8. $r = 10.5$ cm

perimeter of semicircular disc

$$= (\pi r + 2r)$$

$$= \frac{22}{7} \cdot 10.5 + 2 \times 10.5$$

$$= 33 + 21 = 54 \text{ cm}$$

9.

∴ $\qquad D \rightarrow (4, 2)$

10.
$$(F - 1) = 8(s - 1)$$

∴ $\qquad\qquad F - 1 = 8s - 8$

∴ $\qquad\qquad 8s - F = 7 \qquad \ldots(i)$

Now, $F = s^2$, putting this value in eq. (i)

$$8s - s^2 = 7$$

or $\qquad s^2 - 8s + 7 = 0$

or $\qquad s^2 - s - 7s + 7 = 0$

or $\quad s(s - 1) - 7(s - 1) = 0$

or $\quad (s-7)(s-1) = 0$

$\therefore \qquad s = 7 \text{ or } 1$

But it could not be 1 yr because then it will not fulfill the conditions.

$\therefore \qquad s = 7$

11.

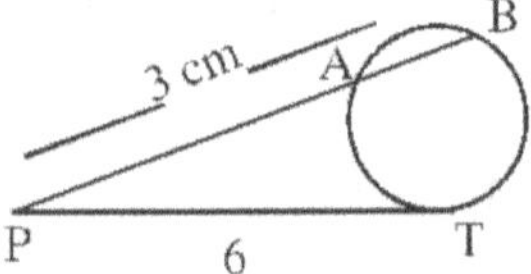

$$PA \cdot PB = PT^2$$

$\Rightarrow \qquad 3(3 + x) = 36$

$\Rightarrow \qquad x = 9$

$\therefore \qquad PB = 3 + 9$

$\qquad = 12 \text{ cm.}$

12. Total no. of Red & White ball = 10

Total no. of ball = 15

Probability of extracting Red or white ball

$$= \frac{10}{15} = \frac{2}{5}$$

13. nth term of A.P. is given by

$$a_n = a + (n-1)\,d \text{ where,}$$

a is first term and d is comm. diff.

$$a_4 = a + (4-1)\,d$$

$$a_4 = a + 3d$$

from question,

$$4(a + 3d) = 7a$$

or $\qquad 4a + 12d = 7a$

or $\qquad 3a = 12d$

$$a = 4d$$

$\therefore$ ratio of first term to comm. diff.

$$\frac{a}{d} = \frac{4d}{d} = 4 : 1$$

14. Vol. of cone $= \dfrac{1}{3}\pi r^2 h$

$$2\pi r = 44$$

$\therefore \qquad r = \dfrac{44}{2} \cdot \dfrac{7}{22} = 7$

$\therefore \qquad \text{Vol} = \dfrac{1}{3} \cdot \dfrac{22}{7} \times 7 \times 7 \times 9$

$$= 462 \text{ m}^3$$

18.

area of square $= \dfrac{1}{2}$ diagonal^2

$$= \frac{1}{2}(2r)^2 = \frac{1}{2} \cdot 4r^2 = 2r^2$$

19.
$$1 \times 3 = 3$$
$$3 \times 3 = 9$$
$$9 \times 3 = \boxed{27}$$
$$27 \times 3 = 81$$

20. All are vowels.

21. 1, 2, 6, 24, 120, $\boxed{720,}$

$\times 2 \quad \times 3 \quad \times 4 \quad \times 5 \quad \times 6$

22. 37, 47, 58, $\boxed{68,}$ 79, 89,

$+10 \quad +11 \quad +10 \quad +11 \quad +10$

23. 1221, 2442, 3663, 4884, $\boxed{6105,}$

$\times 2 \quad \times 3 \quad \times 4 \quad \times 5$

24. L U N C H $\qquad\qquad$ D I N N E R

+3 +2 +3 +2 +3 $\qquad\qquad$ +3 +2 +3 +2 +3 +2

O W Q E K $\qquad\qquad$ G K Q P H T

25. A U T H E N T I C $\qquad$ G E N U I N E

A V T I E O T J C $\qquad$ G F N V I O E

26. S M E L L $\qquad\qquad$ O D O U R

+3 $\qquad\qquad$ +3

P P B O I $\qquad\qquad$ L G L X O

RRB—Railway Recruitment Board

Assistant Loco Pilot (ALP) & Technicians,

Recruitment Examination

FIRST STAGE COMPUTER BASED TEST (CBT)

1. If $4x^3 + 3x^2 + 2x + 4$ is divided by $x + 1$, the remainder will be
   A. 13
   B. 1
   C. –1
   D. –13

2. 20% of 150 is the same as
   A. 10% of 75
   B. 40% of 300
   C. 40% of 75
   D. 30% of 225

3. Two successive discounts of 10% and 20% on a commodity are equal to a total discount of
   A. 30%
   B. 32%
   C. 25%
   D. 28%

4. $x : y : : m : n$ is the same as
   A. $x : n : : y : m$
   B. $x : n : : m : y$
   C. $x : m : : y : n$
   D. $x : m : : n : y$

5. The LCM of $(a^4 - b^4)$ and $(a^2 - b^2)^2$ is
   A. $(a^2 - b^2)$
   B. $(a^2 - b^2)^2$
   C. $(a^2 - b^2)^2 \ (a^4 - b^4)$ D. $(a^2 - b^2)^2 \ (a^2 + b^2)$

6. The equation whose roots are half the roots of the equation $x^2 + 3x + 2 = 0$ is
   A. $2x^2 + 3x + 1 = 0$
   B. $2x^2 + 3x - 1 = 0$
   C. $x^2 + 6x + 8 = 0$
   D. $x^2 + 6x - 8 = 0$

7. The distance between the points $(1, 2)$ and $(1, -1)$ is
   A. $\sqrt{13}$
   B. 3
   C. 1
   D. $\sqrt{5}$

8. A sequence is in Arithmetic Progression. If the first term of the sequence is 5 and the common difference is 4, then the 10th term is
   A. 45
   B. 41
   C. 35
   D. 31

9. Peter's annual income from salary in the year 2002–2003 is ₹ 3,20,000. He makes a saving of ₹ 50,000 in specified forms. The rebate in income tax on account of savings will be
   A. ₹ 10,500
   B. ₹ 10,000
   C. ₹ 7,500
   D. Nil

10. If P is the principal and r is the rate of interest per annum compounded after every x months, then the amount at the end of y years will be

    A. $P\left(1 + \dfrac{r.x}{100}\right)^{xy}$

    B. $P\left(1 + \dfrac{r.x/12}{100}\right)^{12y/x}$

    C. $P\left(1 + \dfrac{x/12}{r.100}\right)^{12y/x}$

    D. $P\left(1 + \dfrac{r.x}{100}\right)^{12x/y}$

11. Mohan's age is 3 times that of Sohan and Ram is 6 years older than Sohan. If the age of Ram is 24 years, Mohan's age is
    A. 6 years
    B. 10 years
    C. 54 years
    D. 90 years

12. The sides of a triangle are 3 cm, 4 cm and 5 cm. The area of the triangle is
    A. 6 cm^2
    B. 12 cm^2
    C. 15 cm^2
    D. 20 cm^2

(1958) Practice Papers—10

13. If two isosceles triangles have equal vertical angles and their areas are in the ratio 9 : 16, then their heights are in the ratio
A. 4 : 3
B. 3 : 4
C. 16 : 9
D. 9 : 16

14. The sum of the opposite angles of a cyclic quadrilateral would be
A. 360°
B. 90°
C. 180°
D. not definite

15. A circle is inscribed in a square of side 5 cm. The ratio of the perimeter of the square and the circumference of the circle is
A. 10 : 10 π
B. 4 : π
C. 5 : π
D. 120 : 6.25 π

16. $\dfrac{\text{cosec } A}{\text{cosec } A - 1} + \dfrac{\text{cosec } A}{\text{cosec } A + 1}$ is equal to
A. 1
B. $\sec^2 A$
C. $\text{cosec}^2 A$
D. $2 \sec^2 A$

17. The median of the following distribution is

x	0	1	2	3	4	5	6	7	8
f	1	9	26	59	72	52	29	7	1

A. 3
B. 4
C. 59
D. 72

18. Three iron cubes, the lengths of whose sides are 3 cm, 4 cm and 5 cm respectively, are moulded and a new cube is formed. The length of the side of the new cube would be
A. 4 cm
B. 6 cm
C. 12 cm
D. 20 cm

19. Which would be the next number in the series?
8, 15, 29, 57, ?
A. 99
B. 113
C. 103
D. 101

20. Insert the missing number.

35	(78)	40
45	(97)	35
25	(?)	30

A. 66
B. 56
C. 67
D. 71

21. If 8 ÷ 5 = 6425, 9 ÷ 6 = 8136, then 4 ÷ 3 = ?
A. 4421
B. 1690
C. 1609
D. 4381

22. If MOZART = 30, PICASSO = 35; then REMBRANDT = ?
A. 40
B. 45
C. 50
D. 65

23. If the word HYDERABAD is written as IZEFSBCBE in code, then AMRITSAR could be written as
A. BNTHUTBS
B. BNSJUTBS
C. BLQHSRBT
D. CNSFUTBS

24. Hemant is older than Chittaranjan. Vikas is older than Shridhar. Mallika is not as old as Vikas but is older than Chittaranjan. Shridhar is not as old as Chittaranjan. Who is the youngest?
A. Hemant
B. Chittaranjan
C. Shridhar
D. Mallika

25. Find the missing in the following.
ACEG : DFHJ : : QSUV : ?
A. TVXY
B. MNPR
C. OQST
D. KMNP

Directions (Qs. 26 and 27): *Read the following statements carefully.*
(1) All P and X are N.
(2) All N except P are X.
(3) No P are M.
(4) No R and N.
(5) All M are either X or R.
(6) No Q are X.

26. Which of the following statements must be true if the above six statements are true?
(*i*) No R are P
(*ii*) Some X and P
(*iii*) Some X are M
A. (*i*) only
B. (*i*) and (*ii*) only
C. (*i*) and (*iii*) only
D. (*i*), (*ii*) and (*iii*), all the three

27. Which of the following must be *false* given the conditions as stated?
A. No Q are P
B. Some Q are neither N nor R
C. Some R are X
D. All R are M

28. The pair of words given here has a definite relationship. Find out from the given options the pair with the similar relationship.

Ecstasy : Gloom

A. congratulation : occasion
B. diligent : successful
C. measure : scale
D. humiliation : exaltation

29. Find the odd one out.

A. ANW   B. DPU
C. GRT   D. JTQ

30.

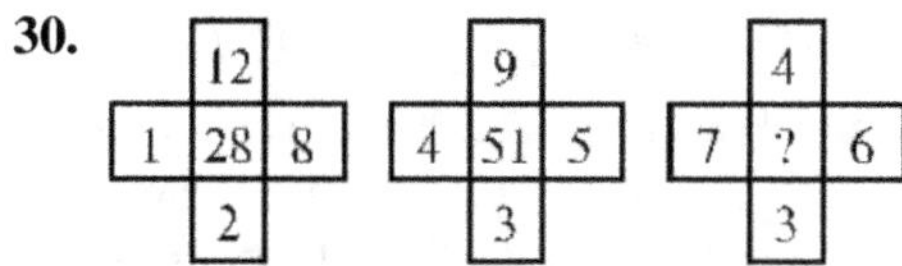

A. 36   B. 46
C. 38   D. 26

31.

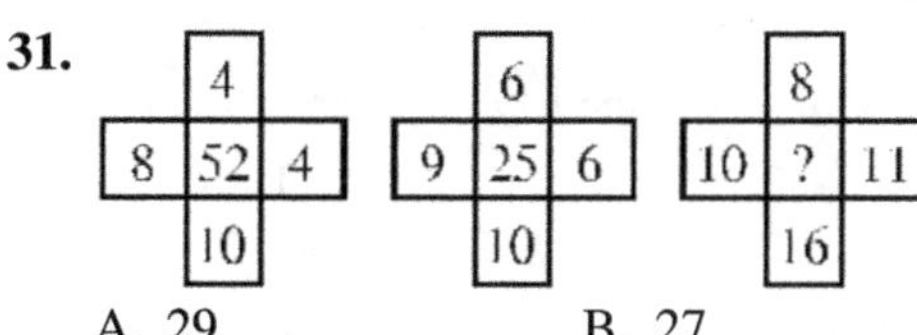

A. 29   B. 27
C. 31   D. 35

32. A motor cycle costs ₹ 40,000 when its is brand new. At the end of each year it is worth 4/5 of what it was at the beginning of the year. What is the motor cycle worth when it is 3 years old?

A. ₹ 16,000
B. ₹ 25,600
C. ₹ 20,480
D. ₹ 24,820

33. Which of the following represents a meaningful order of the given words?

1. elected
2. nomination
3. voting
4. oath-taking
5. canvassing

A. 5 2 1 3 4
B. 5 2 3 1 4
C. 2 5 3 1 4
D. 2 3 1 5 4

Directions (Qs. 34–36): *Which figure will follow next in the sequence?*

34.

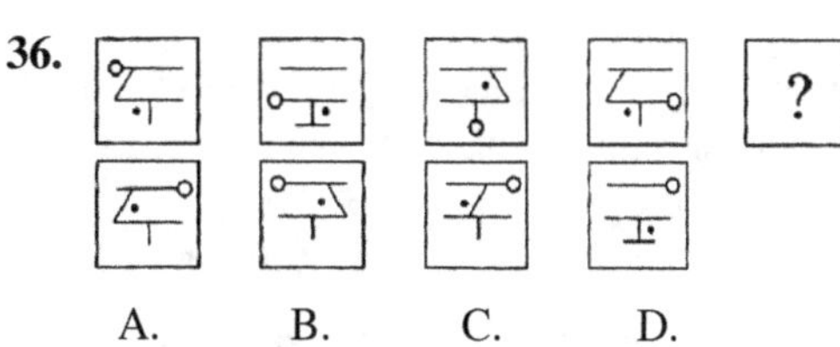

A.   B.   C.   D.

35.

A.   B.   C.   D.

36.

A.   B.   C.   D.

37. The carriers of genetic information are
A. Proteins
B. Lipids and Minerals
C. Nucleic acids
D. Carbohydrates

38. Wind velocity is measured by
A. Anemometer   B. Hydrometer
C. Barometer   D. Hygrometer

39. The causative organism of rabies disease is
A. Bacterium   B. Virus
C. Fungus   D. Algae

40. Which of the following is *not* a plant product?
A. Cotton   B. Lac
C. Jute   D. Sugar

41. Which vitamin in blood plays an important role in clotting?
A. Vitamin A   B. Vitamin D
C. Vitamin E   D. Vitamin K

42. The digestion of starch in the diet starts in the
A. Liver   B. Stomach
C. Intestine   D. Mouth

43. Vitamin C is chemically known as
A. Ascorbic acid
B. Aspartic acid
C. Citric acid
D. Tartaric acid

44. Which one of the following radiations is most penetrating?
A. X-rays
B. Alpha rays
C. Beta rays
D. Gamma rays

45. An atom with an electronic configuration 2, 8, 8 has a valency of
A. −1   B. Zero
C. +1   D. +8

46. Which of the following elements forms the largest number of compounds?
A. Hydrogen   B. Oxygen
C. Silicon   D. Carbon

47. Which of the following gases has lowest density?
A. Argon   B. Helium
C. Oxygen   D. Nitrogen

48. In the formation of Ni^{++}, nickel
A. gains two electrons
B. loses two electrons
C. loses two protons
D. gains two protons

49. If 8.0 g of a metallic oxide on decomposition gives 1·6 g oxygen, what is the equivalent weight of the metal?
A. 8   B. 16
C. 32   D. 64

50. Sphere A attracts Sphere B as well as Sphere C. Sphere B repels Sphere C. If Sphere C is negatively charged it can be concluded that
A. Sphere A is positively charged
B. Sphere A is netagively charged
C. Sphere A is either positively charged or is uncharged
D. Sphere A is either negatively charged or is uncharged

51. The domestic consumption of electricity is calculated in
A. Joules   B. Watts
C. Kilowatt/hour   D. Kilowatt hours

52. The apparent depth of a pond full of water whose real depth is 8 metres will be
A. 2 metres   B. 3 metres
C. 6 metres   D. 8 metres

53. The rays which are *not* deflected by electric or magnetic field are
A. Alpha rays   B. Beta rays
C. Gamma rays   D. Positive rays

54. A metal surface ejects electrons when hit by green light but no electron is ejected when hit by yellow light. The electrons will be ejected when the surface is hit by
A. Blue light   B. Red light
C. Infrared light   D. Heat rays

55. Buddha preached his first sermon at
A. Lumbini   B. Sarnath
C. Varanasi   D. Gaya

56. Meghasthenes visited India during the reign of
A. Harsha
B. Ashoka
C. Chandra Gupta Maurya
D. Kanishka

57. The *Ain-e-Akbari* was written by
A. Farishta   B. Badauni
C. Birbal   D. Abul Fazal

58. Ibn Batuta visited India during the reign of
A. Balban
B. Ala-uddin Khilji
C. Razia
D. Muhammad Bin Tughlaq

59. The Third Battle of Panipat was fought between
A. Britishers and Marathas
B. Marathas and Rajputs
C. Afghans and Sikhs
D. Marathas and Afghans

60. The Quit India Movement was launched in
A. 1930   B. 1940
C. 1942   D. 1946

61. The Partition of Bengal in 1905 was done by
A. Lord Curzon
B. Lord Wellesley
C. Hastings
D. Ripon

62. Which of the following is *not* a Himalayan river?
A. Saryu   B. Alakananda
C. Mandakini   D. Narmada

63. Which is known as the home of the Asiatic lions?
A. Gir National Park
B. Dudhwa National Park
C. Kanha National Park
D. Corbett National Park

64. One of the states through which the Tropic of Cancer passes is
A. Jammu and Kashmir
B. Bihar
C. Himachal Pradesh
D. Jharkhand

65. Which river forms its delta in Odisha?
A. Krishna   B. Mahanadi
C. Godavari   D. Kaveri

66. Which state is the leading producer of red chillies?
A. Punjab   B. Karnataka
C. West Bengal   D. Andhra Pradesh

67. What is Raniganj famous for?
A. Iron ore   B. Coal
C. Manganese   D. Mica

68. The ideals of Liberty, Equality and Fraternity enshrined in the Preamble of the Constitution of India were adopted under inspiration from
A. The Russian Revolution
B. The American Declaration of Independence
C. The U.N. Charter
D. The French Revolution

69. The President of India is
A. the Head of the State
B. the Head of the Government
C. the Head of the Government as well as the State
D. None of the above

70. The Vice President of India is
A. directly elected by the people
B. elected by the same electoral college which elects the President
C. elected by the members of Lok Sabha and Rajya Sabha at a joint meeting
D. elected by the members of Rajya Sabha alone

71. Which one of the following did *not* occupy the office of the Prime Minister?
A. Jagjivan Ram
B. Morarji Desai
C. Chandra Shekhar
D. Both (A) and (C)

72. The Official Language of India is
A. English   B. Hindi
C. Tamil   D. Urdu

73. Where is the World's tallest structure being constructed?
A. Shanghai   B. Dubai
C. New York   D. Guangzhou

74. If 'A ₹ B' means 'A is the father of B', 'A @ B' means 'A is the mother of B', 'A ! B' means 'A is the wife of B', then which of the following means 'T is the grandmother of U'?
A. T @ R ₹ y ! U   B. T @ S ₹ U ! y
C. T @ R ! S ! U   D. None of these

75. Three views of a cube following a particular motion are given below:

What is the letter opposite to A?
A. M   B. P
C. B   D. H

ANSWERS

1	2	3	4	5	6	7	8	9	10
B	C	D	C	D	A	B	B	D	B

11	12	13	14	15	16	17	18	19	20
C	A	B	C	B	D	B	B	B	B

21	22	23	24	25	26	27	28	29	30
C	B	B	C	A	A	C	D	D	B

31	32	33	34	35	36	37	38	39	40
A	C	C	D	A	D	C	A	A	B

41	42	43	44	45	46	47	48	49	50
D	D	A	D	B	D	B	B	B	A

51	52	53	54	55	56	57	58	59	60
C	A	C	A	B	C	D	D	D	C

61	62	63	64	65	66	67	68	69	70
A	D	A	D	B	D	B	D	C	C

71	72	73	74	75
A	B	B	B	D

EXPLANATORY ANSWERS

1. Let $x + 1 = 0$

$\therefore x = -1$

now put the value of x in the given equation

$4x^3 + 3x^2 + 2x + 4$

$= 4(-1)^3 + 3(-1)^2 + 2(-1) + 4$

$= -4 + 3 - 2 + 4 = 1$

2. 20% of 150 = 40% of 75

$$\frac{20}{100} \times 150 = \frac{40}{100} \times 75$$

$$30 = 30$$

3. Let the price be ₹ 100

now the first discount

$$= 100 \times \frac{90}{100} = ₹\,90$$

$$\text{2nd discount} = 90 \times \frac{80}{100} = ₹\,72$$

$$\text{total discount} = 100 - 72 = 28\%$$

5. Let

$$P(x) = a^4 - b^4$$

$$= (a^2)^2 - (b^2)^2$$

$$= (a^2 + b^2)(a^2 - b^2)$$

and

$$z(x) = (a^2 - b^2)^2$$

H.C.F. of $P(x)$ and $Z(x) = a^2 - b^2$

$\therefore$ L.C.M. $P(x)$ and $Z(x)$

$$= \frac{P(x) \times Z(x)}{\text{H.C.F. of } P(x) \text{ and } Z(x)}$$

$$= \frac{(a^2+b^2)(a^2-b^2)(a^2-b^2)^2}{a^2-b^2}$$

$$= (a^2 + b^2)(a^2 - b^2)^2$$

7. Distance between the points

$$= \sqrt{(1-1)^2 + (2-(-1)^2}$$

$$= \sqrt{0^2 + 3^2}$$

$$= 3$$

8.

$$n\text{th term} = a + (n-1)\,d$$
$$= 5 + (10-1)\,4$$
$$= 5 + 36 = 41$$

11. $\because$ Age of Ram = 24 years

$\therefore$ Age of Sohan = 18 years

Since Mohan's age is 3 times that of Sohan

Thus, the age of Mohan

$$= 18 \times 3$$
$$= 54 \text{ years}$$

12. As per data the triangle is right angle triangle $(3^2 + 4^2 = 5^2)$

$\therefore$ Area of right triangle

$$= \frac{1}{2} \times \text{base} \times \text{height}$$
$$= \frac{1}{2} \times 3 \times 4 = 6 \text{ cm}^2$$

15. ABCD is a square with side 5 cm.

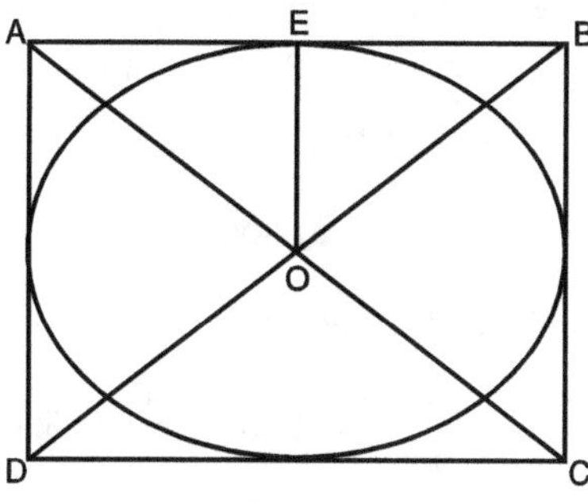

$$BD = AC$$
$$= \text{diagonal of the square}$$

$\therefore$ Area of the square

$$= \frac{1}{2}\,(\text{diagonal})^2 = (\text{side})^2$$
$$\Rightarrow \frac{1}{2}\,(\text{diagonal})^2 = 5 \times 5$$
$$\Rightarrow \text{diagonal} = \sqrt{50}$$
$$\because AC = BD = \sqrt{50}$$
$$\therefore OB = \frac{\sqrt{50}}{2}$$

$\therefore$ By Pythagoras theorem

$$OE = \text{Radius} = \frac{5}{2}$$
$$\therefore \frac{\text{Perimeter of Square}}{\text{Circumference of circle}} = \frac{5 \times 4}{2.\pi.\dfrac{5}{2}} = \frac{4}{\pi}$$

16.

$$\frac{\text{cosec A}}{\text{cosec A} - 1} + \frac{\text{cosec A}}{\text{cosec A} + 1}$$

$$\Rightarrow \frac{\text{cosec A}(\text{cosec A} + 1) + \text{cosec A}(\text{cosec A} - 1)}{\text{cosec}^2 A - 1}$$

$$\Rightarrow \frac{\text{cosec}^2 A + \text{cosec A} + \text{cosec}^2 A - \text{cosec A}}{\text{cosec}^2 A - 1}$$

$$\Rightarrow \frac{2\,\text{cosec}^2 A}{\text{cosec}^2 A - 1} \qquad \Rightarrow \frac{2\,\text{cosec}^2 A}{\cot^2 A}$$

$$\Rightarrow \frac{2\,\text{cosec}^2 A}{\dfrac{\cos^2 A}{\sin^2 A}} \qquad \Rightarrow \frac{2\,\text{cosec}^2 A \cdot \sin^2 A}{\cos^2 A}$$

$$\Rightarrow \frac{2\,\text{cosec}^2 A \cdot \dfrac{1}{\text{cosec}^2 A}}{\cos^2 A}$$

$$= \frac{2}{\cos^2 A} = 2\sec^2 A$$

17.

x	f	$c.f.$
0	1	0
1	9	10
2	26	36
3	59	95
4	72	167
5	52	219
6	29	248
7	7	255
8	1	256

$$N = 256$$

Median = Value of $\left(\dfrac{N+1}{2}\right)$ th item

$$= \frac{256+1}{2} = 128.5 \text{ the item}$$

Hence, the median of group is 4.

18. Total volume of smaller cube

$$= 3^3 + 4^3 + 5^3 = 27 + 64 + 125 = 216$$

$\therefore$ Volume of larger cube $= 216$

$\therefore$ Side of larger cube $= (216)^{1/3} = 6$ c.m.

19. 8   15   29   57   113

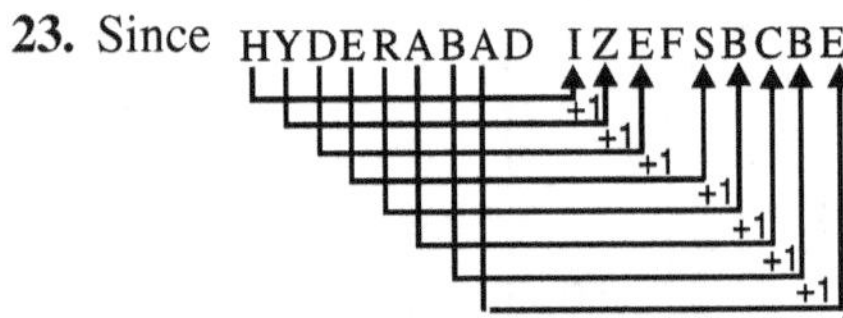

$$+7 \quad +14 \quad +28 \quad +56$$

20. $\because \quad 35 \div 5 = 7 \qquad 40 \div 5 = 8 \qquad 78$

$\qquad \quad 45 \div 5 = 9 \qquad 35 \div 5 = 7 \qquad 97$

$\therefore \quad 25 \div 5 = 5 \qquad 30 \div 5 = 6 \qquad 56$

21. $\qquad 8 \div 5 = 8^2 + 5^2 = 6425$

$\qquad 9 \div 6 = 9^2 + 6^2 = 8136$

$\qquad 4 \div 3 = 4^2 + 3^2 = 1609$

22. MOZART = 30

$\Rightarrow$ number of letter in this word $\times 5$

$$= 6 \times 5 = 30$$

PICASSO = 35

$\Rightarrow$ number of letter in this word $\times 5$

$$= 7 \times 5 = 35$$

REMBRANDT

$\Rightarrow$ number of letter in this word $\times 5$

$$= 9 \times 5 = 45$$

23. Since

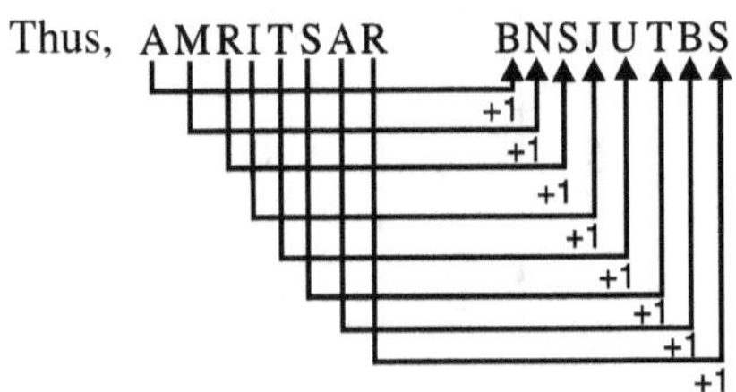

Thus,

24. Hemant > Chittranjan   I

Vikas > Shridhar   II

Vikas > Mallika > Chittranjan   III

Chittranjan > Shridhar   IV

from all the equations

Hemant > Vikas > Mallika > Chittranjan > Shridhar

Thus, Shridhar is youngest.

25.

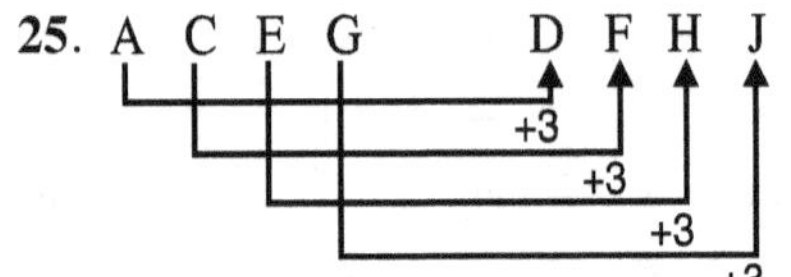

Thus

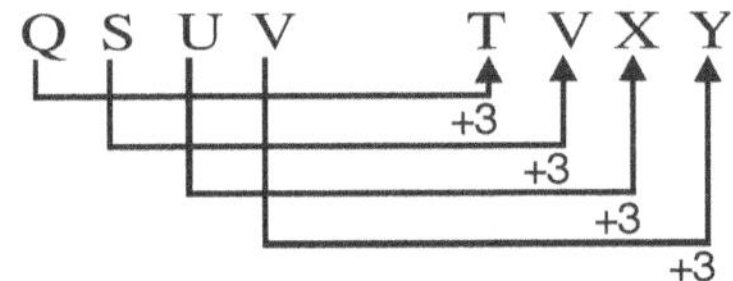

30. $\qquad 1 \times 12 + 8 \times 2 = 12 + 16 = 28$

$\qquad 9 \times 4 + 5 \times 3 = 36 + 15 = 51$

$\qquad 7 \times 4 + 6 \times 3 = 28 + 18 = 46$

32. Price at the end of 1st year

$$= 40000 \times \frac{4}{5} = 32000$$

Price at the end of 2nd year

$$= 32000 \times \frac{4}{5} = 25600$$

$\therefore$ Price at the end of 3rd year

$$= 25600 \times \frac{4}{5} = 20480$$

33. Only option 3 represent the meaningful order.

34. "O" figure moves one step clockwise, "↑" figure follows it and "↑" also moves 90° clockwise in itself. So only option D is satisfying this rule.